DATE DUE JUN 0 4

GAYLORD			PRINTED IN U.S.A.

Hillary Rodham Clinton

These and other titles are included in The Importance Of biography series:

Maya Angelou
Louis Armstrong
Neil Armstrong
Lucille Ball
The Beatles
Alexander Graham Bell
Napoleon Bonaparte
Fidel Castro
Leonardo da Vinci
James Dean
Walt Disney
F. Scott Fitzgerald
Henry Ford
Anne Frank
Mohandas Gandhi
John Glenn
Martha Graham
Ernest Hemingway
Adolf Hitler
Thomas Jefferson
John F. Kennedy

Bruce Lee
Lenin
John Lennon
Abraham Lincoln
Charles Lindbergh
Paul McCartney
Mother Teresa
Muhammad
John Muir
Richard Nixon
Pablo Picasso
Edgar Allan Poe
Queen Elizabeth I
Jonas Salk
Margaret Sanger
Dr. Seuss
William Shakespeare
Frank Sinatra
J.R.R. Tolkien
Simon Wiesenthal
The Wright Brothers

THE IMPORTANCE OF

Hillary Rodham Clinton

by Jim Gullo

LUCENT BOOKS ®

THOMSON

™

GALE

San Diego • Detroit • New York • San Francisco • Cleveland • New Haven, Conn. • Waterville, Maine • London • Munich

© 2004 by Lucent Books. Lucent Books is an imprint of The Gale Group, Inc.,
a division of Thomson Learning, Inc.

Lucent Books® and Thomson Learning™ are trademarks used herein under license.

For more information, contact
Lucent Books
27500 Drake Rd.
Farmington Hills, MI 48331-3535
Or you can visit our Internet site at http://www.gale.com

LIBRARY OF CONGRESS CATALOGING-IN-PUBLICATION DATA

Gullo, Jim, 1957–
   Hillary Rodham Clinton / by Jim Gullo.
p. cm. — (The importance of)
Summary: A biography of the New York senator and wife of the forty-second president
of the United States.
Includes bibliographical references and index.
   ISBN 1-59018-310-X (hardback)
   1. Clinton, Hillary Rodham—Juvenile literature. 2. Presidents' spouses—United
States—Biography—Juvenile literature. 3. Legislators—United States—Biography—Juve-
nile literature. 4. United States. Congress. Senate—Biography—Juvenile literature. [1.
Clinton, Hillary Rodham. 2. First ladies. 3. Legislators. 4. Women—Biography.]
   I. Title. II. Series.
   E887.C55G85 2004
   973.929'092—dc21

                                                                       2003003539

Printed in the United States of America

Contents

Foreword

THE IMPORTANCE OF biography series deals with individuals who have made a unique contribution to history. The editors of the series have deliberately chosen to cast a wide net and include people from all fields of endeavor. Individuals from politics, music, art, literature, philosophy, science, sports, and religion are all represented. In addition, the editors did not restrict the series to individuals whose accomplishments have helped change the course of history. Of necessity, this criterion would have eliminated many whose contribution was great, though limited. Charles Darwin, for example, was responsible for radically altering the scientific view of the natural history of the world. His achievements continue to impact the study of science today. Others, such as Chief Joseph of the Nez Percé, played a pivotal role in the history of their own people. While Joseph's influence does not extend much beyond the Nez Percé, his nonviolent resistance to white expansion and his continuing role in protecting his tribe and his homeland remain an inspiration to all.

These biographies are more than factual chronicles. Each volume attempts to emphasize an individual's contributions both in his or her own time and for posterity. For example, the voyages of Christopher Columbus opened the way to European colonization of the New World. Unquestionably, his encounter with the New World brought monumental changes to both Europe and the Americas in his day. Today, however, the broader impact of Columbus's voyages is being critically scrutinized. *Christopher Columbus,* as well as every biography in The Importance Of series, includes and evaluates the most recent scholarship available on each subject.

Each author includes a wide variety of primary and secondary source quotations to document and substantiate his or her work. All quotes are footnoted to show readers exactly how and where biographers derive their information, as well as provide stepping-stones to further research. These quotations enliven the text by giving readers eyewitness views of the life and times of each individual covered in The Importance Of series.

Finally, each volume is enhanced by photographs, bibliographies, chronologies, and comprehensive indexes. For both the casual reader and the student engaged in research, The Importance Of biographies will be a fascinating adventure into the lives of people who have helped shape humanity's past and present, and who will continue to shape its future.

IMPORTANT DATES IN THE LIFE OF HILLARY RODHAM CLINTON

1975
Bill and Hillary are married on October 11.

1972
Hillary and Bill campaign for George McGovern.

1937
Hugh Rodham leaves Scranton, Pennsylvania, for Chicago, where he meets Dorothy Howell.

1950
The Rodham family moves to Park Ridge, Illinois.

1969
Life magazine names Hillary as a student leader. She enters Yale Law School.

1935	1945	1955	1965	1975

1947
Hillary Rodham is born on October 26 in a Chicago hospital.

1965
Hillary graduates from high school and enters Wellesley College in Massachusetts.

1970
Hillary meets Bill Clinton.

1974
Hillary joins the Watergate investigation team; arrives in Fayetteville, Arkansas.

1977
Hillary begins working at Rose Law Firm; she is appointed chairperson of the Legal Services Corporation by President Jimmy Carter.

1992
Bill Clinton elected president; Hillary becomes first lady of nation.

1994
Congress authorizes Whitewater investigation.

1978
Bill becomes governor of Arkansas and Hillary is first lady.

1996
Bill Clinton wins reelection to second term as president; Hillary publishes *It Takes a Village: And Other Lessons Children Teach Us.*

1983
Bill reelected as governor of Arkansas; holds office for next ten years; Hillary appointed to head statewide Education Standards Committee.

1998
House votes to impeach Bill Clinton for lying and obstructing justice in Lewinsky scandal.

1980   **1985**   **1990**   **1995**   **2005**

1993
Hugh Rodham dies; Hillary appointed to head Health Care Task Force; delivers 1,342-page plan to Congress.

2001
Hillary returns to Washington to begin her six-year term in U.S. Senate.

1988
Hillary named to list of America's 100 Most Powerful Lawyers.

2000
Hillary is elected senator of New York.

1999
Bill and Hillary establish residency in New York State.

1995
Hillary speaks at United Nations Fourth World Conference on Women in Beijing, China.

1980
Chelsea Victoria Clinton is born on February 27.

1997
Hillary hosts White House conferences on child care.

A First Lady Like No Other

You know, you have a choice, whatever your circumstances are. You either become overwhelmed by life or you continue to try to challenge yourself to grow and enjoy the days that you're given—and that has always been the way I've lived.

—Hillary Rodham Clinton

On a cool day in the nation's capital in December 2000, First Lady Hillary Rodham Clinton did something that no first lady has ever done in the history of the American presidency. Accompanied by her usual secret service escort and trailed by a pack of reporters, Hillary made the short trip from the White House to Capitol Hill in Washington, D.C., for an orientation dubbed "Senate School." The day-long seminar in getting familiar with the U.S. Senate was not meant for first ladies but for new senators who had recently been elected and were about to begin their terms. Hillary Clinton, who had lived in the White House for eight tumultuous years, was now Senator Clinton of New York State, an office that she had won in a landslide in the November 2000 elections.

Her new position was just one of many firsts for Hillary Rodham Clinton. Not only was she the first first lady in the history of the country to run for and win elected office, she was also the first woman elected to a statewide office in the state of New York. As a successful lawyer who had served on many legal and corporate boards, she was the most career-oriented woman who had ever lived in the White House. During Bill Clinton's presidency, she was the first first lady to serve on high-level presidential commissions, and when scandal rocked the presidency, she was the first first lady to be ordered to the courtroom to answer questions about her past.

A LIFELONG TRAILBLAZER

Blazing new trails for women was something that Hillary had been doing all of her life. As a college student in Massachusetts she had worked to change things for the better on her campus and in society in general. She was the first student ever asked to speak at Wellesley College's graduation ceremonies; her speech, in which she called for "more immediate, ecstatic and penetrating modes of living,"[1] was hailed across the country as the fresh voice of a new generation. As a young lawyer, she helped draft criminal charges against President Richard M. Nixon, which led to his resignation in the Watergate scandal. While her husband was governor of Arkansas, she became a national advocate on behalf of women and children, a role that she took to an international scale when she became first lady of the nation.

She has written books that have been read by millions of people, given speeches before world bodies, and been instrumental in directing the successful presidential campaigns that landed Bill Clinton in the White House for two successful terms. She was named one of the 100 Most Influential Lawyers in America twice, was appointed chairperson of the Legal Services Corporation by President Jimmy Carter in 1977, and chaired the prestigious Children's Defense Fund for three years in the 1980s. She was instrumental in revamping the educational system in Arkansas while her husband was governor, and as first lady she helped push through legislation on gun control, assault weapons, and children's health insurance.

Throughout her long career in politics, she has struggled to maintain the image and carry out the traditional duties of a first lady—first in Arkansas and then in Washington, D.C. She has been the doting mother to Chelsea Clinton, whom she helped raise to adulthood in the most glaring of public spotlights, and she has been a supportive wife even under the most trying of circumstances.

A LIGHTNING ROD FOR CRITICISM

Along with the accolades, Hillary Rodham Clinton has endured a great deal of criticism. It started when Bill ran for reelection as governor in Arkansas and his opponents publicly castigated Hillary, the working wife and lawyer. It continued when Bill ran for president with Hillary at his side as an adviser, a "two-for-one presidency" to which many Americans objected. It reached a fever pitch when

HILLARY SYMBOLIZED THE WOMEN OF HER GENERATION IN MANY WAYS

As first lady, Hillary represented many things to many people, as author Michael Tomasky reports in Hillary's Turn, *his book about her successful campaign for the U.S. Senate in New York:*

"Hillary Clinton has existed primarily as a symbol, both to those who admire her and to those who detest her. She was either a role model for a new kind of first lady and a touchstone for feminism's triumph, or she was an unreconstructed flower child and a threat to the social order."

Clinton took office in 1992. The public—and particularly the press—grew suspicious of Hillary's influence inside the White House and demanded to know how much power she actually wielded. "Impeach Hillary!" was the message of the day on many bumper stickers across America.

Finally, Hillary's personal life and role as a wife were painfully laid open and dissected by the press and the public when scandals rocked the White House over the president's infidelity. A sexual relationship that the president had with an intern wound up crippling the Clinton administration and the Democratic Party in the final year of Bill Clinton's presidency. At first Hillary staunchly defended her husband and lashed out at his accusers. When it became clear that the accusations were true, she did not publicly approve nor condemn his actions but refused to let the scandal destroy her marriage or her personal dignity.

WHO IS THE TRUE HILLARY?

Hillary Rodham Clinton's very name evokes the strongest of responses in peo-

Hillary Rodham Clinton is sworn in as senator of New York on January 3, 2001. Her win in New York made Hillary the first first lady in America's history to win an elected office.

WHY HILLARY WAS VIEWED AS A LIGHTNING ROD

In an interview on the Today Show when she was first lady, Hillary reflected on the attention that was focused on her as a kind of lightning rod of discussion about women's roles in society:

"Because I think women's roles right now are lightning rods every day in so many different ways. In workplaces and kitchens, and places all over America, people are struggling to define what it means to be a woman, a mother, a wife—all of the different roles that we play. And because my husband is the first of our generation to be elected president, it's the first time that a lot of those private discussions have really been played out at such a very high and visible point in our public life."

ple. "Her admirers see her as their courageous field general in the values war," wrote one journalist who covered Hillary's Senate campaign in New York. "Her detractors see in her a madly ambitious woman who lusts for personal power."[2] There are some who consider Hillary Clinton to be the most remarkable woman of her generation. Many others consider her to be a symbol of all that they consider wrong with modern American life.

Indeed, it is hard to imagine any other person in political life who is the subject of such powerful and passionate reactions. To many conservative Americans, Hillary Clinton evokes a series of negative images: staunch liberal who wants the government to take over the raising of their children and the management of their health care; former campus activist who railed against the government; power-mad wife who secretly tried to take over the reins of the government from her husband and nearly succeeded; ultrafeminist who sneered at traditional women's roles as wife and mother and tried to convince every woman in the country to leave the house and get a job.

To her supporters she shines as an example of a woman who has balanced career and family, politics and marriage and has achieved remarkable things. Whatever Hillary Clinton's legacy, it is a legacy still in the making.

Chapter 1

A Daughter of High Expectations

My parents gave me my belief in working hard, doing well in school and not being limited by the fact that I was a little girl.

—Hillary Rodham Clinton

Senator Hillary Rodham Clinton has always been quick to praise her parents, Hugh and Dorothy Rodham, not only for allowing her to have big dreams but for pushing her to do her best to fulfill those dreams. Even in the 1950s, when most girls were expected to become housewives, the Rodhams encouraged Hillary to set very high goals for herself. Hillary would later say, "As a girl growing up in the forties and fifties, to have both a mother and a father who basically said, 'You can do or be whatever you choose, as long as you're willing to work for it,' was an unusual message."[3]

FATHER HUGH ESCAPES THE MINES

That message was forged in the dangerous coal mines of Scranton, Pennsylvania, the tough, working-class town where Hugh Rodham grew up during the Great Depression of the 1930s. His grandfather had come to America from his native Wales in Great Britain to dig coal, and as a young man, Hugh briefly tried his hand at mining when jobs were scarce. He put in just enough time in the mines to realize that he did not want to spend his entire working life underground in a hot, treacherous mine shaft. Fortunately for Hugh, his father had escaped the mines by working for Scranton Lace Works, a company that manufactured curtain and lace products. When Hugh returned to Scranton in 1935 after graduating from Penn State University, he took a job with his father's company and began to learn the business of making and selling draperies.

Hugh liked the work, and in 1937 he was offered a job as a salesman for a large, successful drapery company in Chicago. He left Scranton behind with the hope of starting his own curtain business one day and raising a family in better conditions than he had known as a child. Years later he would take Hillary and her two brothers back to Scranton to show them the bleak coal mine where he had once worked. He wanted his children to see firsthand the kind of life they might have had if he had chosen to stay in the mines rather than go to college.

HILLARY IS BORN IN CHICAGO

Dorothy Howell was born in Chicago, but her life was disrupted at the age of eight when her parents divorced and she was sent to live with relatives in California. She grew up there, but by her midteens she left the home of a stern, unloving grandmother and began working to earn her own room and board. She made her way back to Chicago and in 1937 applied for a job as a secretary at the Columbia Lace Company, where Hugh worked. There the two met. They began to date and were married in 1942, just after America entered World War II. Hugh joined the navy and was sent to train sailors for combat.

When the war ended, the young couple moved into a one-bedroom apartment on the north side of Chicago. Hugh established his own curtain and drapery business in the city and worked long hours to make it successful.

On October 26, 1947, their first child was born at Edgewater Hospital. The baby girl weighed eight pounds, eight ounces, and she was given a name that was intentionally meant by her parents to

Dorothy Rodham, Hugh Rodham, and Hillary dine together in 1992. Both of Hillary's parents were hard workers who had high expectations of their first child.

be unique. "Dorothy wanted her [daughter's] name to be something different," writes author Donnie Radcliffe, "so she chose Hillary because besides having family significance it was often given to boys. Dorothy liked that."[4]

When Hillary was two months old, her parents took her to Scranton to be christened in the Court Street Methodist Church, where Hugh had worshiped as a child. It was the beginning of a religious faith and commitment to Methodism that stayed with her throughout her life.

A Move to the Suburbs

The Rodham family grew to four with the birth of Hillary's brother Hugh in 1950 (youngest brother Tony was born four years later), and Hugh and Dorothy decided to move their family out of the city. They found a handsome, three-bedroom brick house in the suburb of Park Ridge, Illinois, a small town of neat, orderly homes and green lawns. From there Hugh commuted into Chicago every day to conduct his business; Dorothy stayed home with their children. In Park Ridge they could realize their dream of raising a family in a peaceful town.

Park Ridge had all of the trappings of middle-class success. It was clean, safe, and quiet. There were several playing fields and parks, and the streets were free of traffic. Children in the neighborhood could play outside and ride their bikes. The school system was rated highly, and the Methodist church that the Rodhams joined was prosperous and active.

The population of Park Ridge was mostly white and very conservative. There was not a single student of African American descent in Hillary's schools until she reached twelfth grade. In most elections Park Ridge residents overwhelmingly voted Republican. It was a place for people who wanted to fit in and accept the rules laid down by the majority; nonconformity or even diversity of views was not tolerated or accepted.

Hillary as a Little Girl

For Hillary and her brothers, though, Park Ridge was like a huge playground filled with friends. "There must have been forty or fifty children within a four-block radius of our house and within four years of Hillary's age," Dorothy Rodham once explained. "They were all together, all the time, a big extended family. There were more boys than girls, lots of playing and competition. [Hillary] held her own at cops-and-robbers, hide-and-seek, chase-and-run."[5]

Besides the games and fun, however, young Hillary learned an important lesson about standing up for herself. Shortly after moving to Park Ridge, she encountered a girl named Suzy who was known throughout the neighborhood for bullying both boys and girls with cruel words and fists. Sure enough, after she sent young Hillary home crying one day, Hillary was afraid to go back outside and play with the other children. As author Gail Sheehy reports, it was a defining moment for the future first

An Unfortunate Coincidence

Bill and Hillary Clinton might have grown up in the same neighborhood if not for a terrible accident. Author Donnie Radcliffe explains in Hillary Rodham Clinton: A First Lady for Our Time:

"In one of those geographical coincidences, the Rodhams lived for a time at 5722 North Winthrop in the Edgewater area of Chicago, not all that far from the home Bill Clinton's father, William Blythe, had bought for his wife, Virginia, and the child they were expecting. . . . Three months before Bill was born—and seventeen months before Hillary was born—Blythe was killed three miles west of Sikeston, Missouri, when his fast-moving car apparently blew a tire and skidded off the road. He was on his way to pick up Virginia in Hope, Arkansas, and take her back to Chicago in time for the birth of their child."

lady, who, with the encouragement of her mother, went back outside to deal with Suzy:

"There's no room in this house for cowards," Mrs. Rodham declared. . . . "You're going to have to stand up to her. The next time she hits you, I want you to hit her back." Out trudged the trembling four-year old. A circle of scowling boys and the pugilistic [inclined to fight] girl closed around her. Suddenly Hillary threw out her fist, knocking Suzy off her pins. The boys' mouths dropped open. Flushed with victory, Hillary ran home and exclaimed to her proud mother: "I can play with the boys now!"[6]

With her place in the group of neighborhood children secured, Hillary flourished. Her early childhood was filled with play and learning. Every Christmas Eve she helped Dorothy bake chocolate chip cookies, an annual Rodham tradition. In grade school Hillary was a bright student who liked to ask questions. She especially enjoyed field trips into the city to see the skeletons of dinosaurs and other natural attractions at Chicago's Field Museum.

Hugh's Demanding Style of Parenting

As she got older, Hillary joined the Girl Scouts, where she earned several emblems and merit badges. She learned how to play cards and softball and became a fan of professional baseball. Hillary liked baseball so much that she studied statistics and baseball history and could rattle off seemingly obscure information like the entire batting order of the 1927 New York Yankees. As a softball

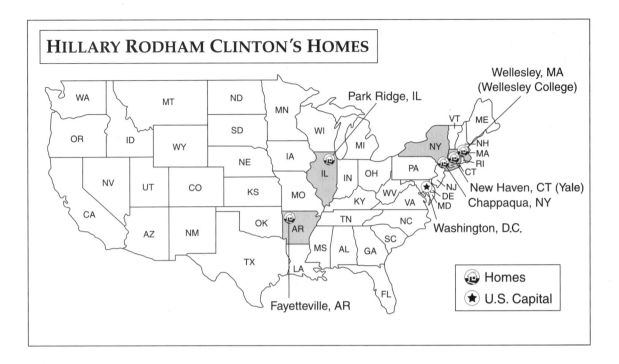

HILLARY RODHAM CLINTON'S HOMES

Wellesley, MA
(Wellesley College)

Park Ridge, IL

New Haven, CT (Yale)

Chappaqua, NY

Washington, D.C.

Fayetteville, AR

🏠 Homes
★ U.S. Capital

player she was a better-than-average shortstop and a good fielder, but she had a hard time hitting. Hugh, who had majored in physical education in college and could be a tough taskmaster, took her to the park and pitched to her for hours, demanding that she do better until she began to hit the ball hard.

Hugh could be brusque and demanding, and he had a confrontational style of communicating with his children. As Hillary recalled, his stern reach extended far beyond the boundaries of their house and yard. "I didn't run afoul of my parents very often," she wrote. "They were strict about my respecting authority, and not just parental authority. My father's favorite saying was: 'You get in trouble at school, you get in trouble at home.'"[7]

Hugh Rodham gave praise sparingly; he was more likely to find fault or criticize in an

attempt to motivate his children to succeed. One time Hillary's brother Hugh, an accomplished football quarterback, completed nine out of ten passes and led his team to victory. But his father only commented on the one pass that was incomplete.

Hillary understood that her father meant well and wanted the best for her. When she was older, she reflected on the strong sense of community that she received from her parents and her teachers, ministers, and neighbors in Park Ridge. "There were always adults around who would care about you and would pick you up when you fell," she said to a magazine reporter. "I mean they might not give you much sympathy, but they would be there for you. And they would tell you to keep going and not get deterred, and I just see so many kids today who don't have that kind of support."[8]

HILLARY'S LOVE FOR EDUCATION AND CHILDREN BEGINS

As Hillary grew into preadolescence, she began to take an active interest in children and education. She began to see ways of integrating her interests, such as sports and learning, with activities that could help people. For example, she was a good swimmer, and during her junior high school years she learned canoeing and water safety. This helped her get work during the summers as a lifeguard at a wading pool for toddlers. She also began to babysit younger children in the neighborhood, and she was active in children's activities at the Methodist church.

Hillary was a good student who enjoyed school. She impressed her teachers and gained a reputation among her classmates as a hard worker who was committed to getting good grades. She once turned in a term paper for a history class that was seventy-five pages long and was accompanied by 150 note cards and fifty bibliography references. But when she brought home straight A's in junior high, Hugh's comment was a sarcastic, "Well, Hillary, that must be an easy school you go to."[9]

HILLARY JOINS "THE UNIVERSITY OF LIFE"

It was at the Methodist church that Hillary met someone who was one of her greatest childhood influences. In 1961, when Hillary was thirteen, a young minister named Don Jones arrived in Park Ridge. Put in charge of the church's youth group, he was determined to take the teachings of the church out of the Sunday school classroom and

---

"WE WOULD JUST RIDE AROUND"

Hillary mourns the passing of a time when children could play outside all day without supervision, as she did growing up in Park Ridge, Illinois. This passage is from The Unique Voice of Hillary Rodham Clinton, *a collection of quotes by the then–first lady edited by Claire G. Osborne:*

"I was thinking one day how I used to get on my bicycle in the morning with my friends, and my mother would say, 'Well, be back in time for dinner.' And we'd go to each other's house; we'd go to the park; we would just ride around. And nobody was concerned about us. They had told us the obvious things about, you know, stay away from strangers and the like. But people expected their children to be safe at the end of the day. And that is practically impossible in most parts of our country now."

---

into the community at large. He wanted to show his students that values like compassion, caring, and helping one's neighbors were not just topics for discussion but values to guide one's whole life. For that reason Jones referred to the youth group as "The University of Life," and he set out to show the youngsters that there was a world far different from safe, sheltered Park Ridge, a world where people were struggling for basic necessities like food, housing, and clothing.

To do this he arranged many trips for his students that took them out of the confines of Park Ridge. On one trip he took Hillary and the youth group into one of the poorest sections of inner-city Chicago to meet with a group of underprivileged children, most of whom were African American. As a way to start the two different groups of youngsters talking, Jones showed them a copy of Pablo Picasso's painting *Guernica*, which depicts war and conflict in an abstract way. The white children from Park Ridge pointed out some of the disturbing images in the painting, but they were unable to make a connection with the painting and their lives. The inner-city children responded differently. The painting drew many emotional responses from them. One young girl got so upset that she cried out, "Why did my uncle have to get shot because he parked in the wrong parking place?"[10]

It was also at this time in her life that Hillary joined a church-organized babysitting service for the migrant farmworkers who picked fruit and vegetables in the nearby orchards of Illinois. She and her friends watched over the children of the workers, most of whom came from Mexico and Latin America, while the parents toiled long hours in the field. She noted the disparities between their lives and hers, and Hillary's social conscience began to take shape.

On another trip conducted by Reverend Don Jones, Hillary began to understand that social awareness could also be connected with politics. When Hillary was fifteen, he took the University of Life students to hear Reverend Martin Luther King Jr. speak at Chicago's Orchestra Hall. Hillary was entranced not only by the message delivered by the great advocate for civil rights but by the sheer strength of his presence. She got to shake his hand at the end of the speech, a moment that she would never forget.

Hillary was developing a sense that she could accomplish anything she set out to do, but she was rudely brought down to Earth at the age of fourteen when she wrote to the new NASA space agency and asked what it would take for her to become an astronaut. They wrote back informing her that women were not being accepted in the astronaut-training program, which made her furious (and which would later change). "I later realized that I couldn't have been an astronaut anyway because I have such terrible eyesight," she would recall. "That somewhat placated me."[11]

Hillary Becomes a Leader in High School

By the time Hillary entered Maine East High School as a freshman in 1961, she

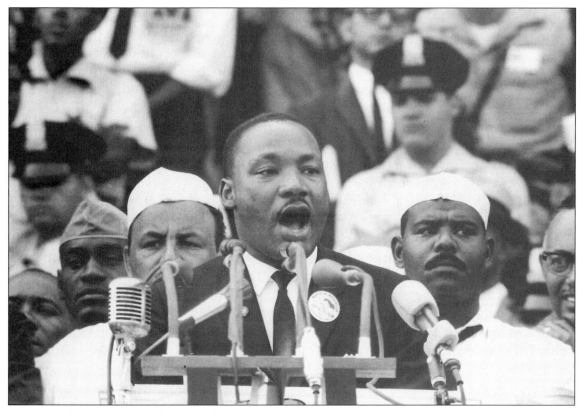

Martin Luther King Jr. speaks in Washington, D.C. King's powerful presence inspired a young Hillary to draw a connection between politics and her budding social conscience.

had already begun to distinguish herself not only as an A student but as a confident and mature young woman. The ethic of hard work that her parents had taught her had become an ingrained part of Hillary's personality. Author Joyce Milton points out that Hillary was the kind of student that teachers love to have in their classrooms. "Articulate and well prepared but not prone to challenge authority, she was the kind of student who makes teaching a pleasure," Milton wrote. "In classroom debates, she could state her opinions in complete sentences, reeling off the main points of her argument in logical order."[12]

Besides studying hard, however, Hillary maintained a busy extracurricular schedule, joining numerous committees, throwing herself into school politics, and enjoying an extensive array of clubs and activities. She loved to argue and debate, and she had no qualms about displaying her intelligence. Hillary would later say, "When I got into high school, I saw a lot of my friends who had been really lively and smart and doing well in school beginning to worry that boys would think they were too smart, or beginning to cut back on how well they did or the courses they took, because that's not where their boyfriends were. And I can recall thinking, 'Gosh—why are they doing that?' It didn't make sense to me."[13]

That kind of attitude impressed her teachers and church leaders, but it put off a lot of her classmates, who found Hillary to be mean and pushy. In addition, she had acquired some of her father's style of making cutting remarks and making other people feel incompetent in her presence. Some classmates even teased her behind her back for always wanting to be in charge of every activity and for acting like she was the only one smart enough to do things right. Despite this she had a lot of friends, seemed to know every kid in school by name, and tried to rally groups of students behind causes that she supported.

By the time she was a junior, Hillary was blossoming into an attractive young woman, with blonde hair and blue eyes and an athletic figure. Yet, unlike her peers at school, who wore the latest fashions, wore makeup, and piled their hair up into tall "beehive" styles, Hillary was uninterested in how she looked or dressed. She wore no makeup, her clothes were plain, and she wore thick eyeglasses to correct her weak vision. She did not date or show much interest in boys, either. Some of the other students admired Hillary's independence in this regard even if they did not appreciate her sometimes brusque attitude. As one classmate pointed out, Hillary "was totally unconcerned about how she appeared to people, and she was loved for that."[14]

HIGH SCHOOL POLITICS

Hillary was the vice president of her junior class, but she suffered her first political defeat later that year when she ran for the presidency of the senior class and lost. She attributed the defeat to cutting remarks that the boys who ran against her made during the campaign. They attacked her personally, and although Hillary felt that she had a better grasp of the issues than the other candidates, the criticism stuck. It was just the beginning of her political education, and it helped Hillary begin to realize that politics was not just about being the smartest or most aggressive candidate but about reaching out to a wide array of people with her message. Speaking at her old high school in 1992, Hillary said, "I firmly believe that the whole purpose of politics . . . is how people get together, how they agree upon their goals, how they move together to realize those goals, how they make the absolutely inevitable tradeoffs between deeply held beliefs that are incompatible."[15]

Hillary's own beliefs of the time show some definite contradictions. On the one hand she embraced the liberal philosophy of civil rights and reaching out to help the poor that she was absorbing from Reverend Don Jones and his University of Life. On the other hand, thanks to her father's political discussions at home and the prevailing mood of Park Ridge, Hillary was an ardent Goldwater girl. She supported and passionately endorsed the politics of conservative Republican senator Barry Goldwater of Arizona. In 1964, during her senior year of high school, Goldwater ran for president against Democrat

Lyndon Baines Johnson. Hillary was busy at school and in the community handing out Goldwater literature, hanging his campaign posters, and fervently defending his policies.

It came as a shock to Hillary that year when a teacher organized a school debate and made Hillary play the role of Johnson instead of her hero Goldwater. She had to stand before the student body and criticize Goldwater's policies while defending Johnson's proposals of extending civil rights to all people and devoting time and money to education and welfare. Hillary apparently was not too convincing, because the students voted for Goldwater in the mock election that followed the debate. In the real election, Johnson was victorious. Years later Hillary joked about her views as a teenager. The Hillary Clinton of today is often castigated by critics for her liberal politics. "How was it that a nice conservative Republican girl from Park Ridge went so wrong?"[16] she joked.

GRADUATING WITH HONORS

When it came time to present the awards to the graduating class of 1965, Hillary repeatedly went to the stage to collect her accolades. She was an A student who finished in the top 5 percent of her class and was a member of the National Honor Society, Speech Activities and Debate, the Girls Athletic Association, and Student Council.

With high school behind her, Hillary was poised to begin a new challenge. Her grades and record of service were good enough that she could have gone to any college in the country, including schools nearby in Chicago, but she chose instead to leave Park Ridge and her family for the East Coast. She had decided to attend Wellesley College in Massachusetts. The school had the reputation for being one of the best and toughest colleges for women in the country.

Hillary would soon find herself in the middle of one of the most important political movements of her time. In

WHY EDUCATION WAS IMPORTANT TO HILLARY

With the encouragement of her parents, Hillary realized early on that education could open doors for her, as she related in The Unique Voice of Hillary Rodham Clinton:

"[My parents] told me it was my obligation to go to school, that I had an obligation to use my mind. They told me that an education would enable me to have a lot more opportunities in life, that if I went to school and took it seriously and studied hard, not only would I learn things and become interested in the world around me, but I would open up all kinds of doors to myself so that, when I was older, I would have some control over my environment."

Hillary Rodham (standing) poses with three Park Ridge High School classmates in 1964. Hillary was a top student at her high school and graduated with honors.

the late 1960s, the United States was at war in Vietnam, and the nation was convulsed by protests against the war, civil rights protests, and a dramatic change in the role of women in American society. College students played a major role in defining the important issues of the day, and for the first time their voices were heard by the people who ran the government. She did not know it when she left her comfortable home behind, but Hillary Rodham was destined to become one of the major spokespersons for her generation.

2 The Making of an Activist

It's an interesting question . . . can one be a mind conservative and a heart liberal?
—*Hillary, in a letter from college*

In the fall of 1965 Hugh and Dorothy packed the family car with their daughter's belongings and headed east, driving nearly one thousand miles to Wellesley, Massachusetts. Hillary handled the transition with her usual confidence and decisiveness, but the move was hard on Dorothy. "It was really, really hard to leave her," she later told a newspaper reporter of delivering her eldest child and only daughter to college. "After we dropped her off, I just crawled in the back seat and cried."[17]

Hillary displayed no such longing for Park Ridge and the safe confines of home. Aside from visits home for holidays and summer vacations in the coming years, she never again lived in the sheltered community of her childhood. According to author Gail Sheehy, Hillary hardly mentioned any pangs of homesickness in letters that she wrote to her friends during her first year of college. Being away from home, and particularly breaking free of the overbearing discipline of

Hugh, had a liberating effect on her. "She mentioned her mother only once," wrote Sheehy. "The few times she referred to her father, it was in the context of developing strategies to elude his oppressive control."[18]

A Commitment to Service

All-women Wellesley College was a nurturing place that prided itself on educating women for a lifetime of service. The college's motto was not to be ministered unto, but to minister. This meant, in other words, that a person should give of oneself and one's service—to the community and society at large—rather than taking. Hillary bristled when one popular magazine singled out Wellesley for turning out well-rounded housewives, but in those days before women could dream about holding political office or running their own companies, they could at least dream about marrying well and living an active life of service. Many of Hillary's classmates came from wealthy East Coast families. They were the daughters of bankers and businessmen, politicians and statesmen. As the elite young women of their era, they were expected to be well educated and bright, as well as graceful, polite members of high society.

With its stately buildings, green lawns, and views of placid Lake Waban, Wellesley seemed removed from the raging issues and conflicts that began to sweep the nation in the mid-1960s. The war in Vietnam had escalated, and people were beginning to question the involvement of America in what seemed to be a regional conflict far away in Asia. As more young American soldiers were drafted and killed in the war, the protests grew more widespread and radical, particularly on college campuses. At the same time, issues of civil rights for minorities led to clashes with police in cities across America and violent race riots in Los Angeles.

The students of Wellesley debated these issues, but their protests were much less strident than on many college campuses. They began to organize and request, rather than demand, changes in some of the long-standing rules of the college that they felt were unfair to students. In Hillary's freshman year, for example, students openly questioned policies of how the college selected roommates and why students could not travel freely off-campus without their parents' permission. Hillary led a group of students who complained about required courses of study that students needed to have in order to meet Wellesley's graduation requirements.

Hillary Rodham (center) listens to the opinions of a fellow Wellesley student during a discussion. At Wellesley, Hillary became very active in student government.

At the same time, the ten African American students on campus formed an association in order to have their own grievances heard. They wanted the administration to admit more African American students and hire more African American professors. It was the first time that Wellesley's black students had joined together to be heard. Hillary became a friend and supporter of the group, and in what passed as a bold personal statement for the times, she invited one of the African American students to attend church with her one Sunday. "Both the college and the country were going through a period of rapid, sometimes tumultuous changes," Hillary later wrote. "My classmates and I felt challenged and, in turn, challenged the college from the moment we arrived. Nothing was taken for granted."[19]

Still loyal to her Park Ridge politics, Hillary joined the campus Republican club in her freshman year, and she was quickly elected to be its president. The students helped campaign for Republican candidates in the Boston area, typing letters, manning phone lines, and going into the community to campaign for the Republican cause. Their efforts that year were successful, as Republican Edward Brooke won a U.S. Senate seat and was sent to Washington, D.C., to represent the state of Massachusetts.

Although she still considered herself to be a Republican, Hillary began to lean away from the politics of the party, preferring politicians who brought more liberal views of how to cope with major issues like race relations and feminism. She decided to become personally involved with government. In her sophomore year her classmates urged her to run for student government and made her their class representative.

A GOOD STUDENT AND FIERCE DEBATER

Hillary was finding herself increasingly interested in government and its role in helping people, and studying political science in college fueled her passion. She studied relentlessly in order to get good grades, and in her spare time she loved to read and debate politics with her friends. She was known for leading a group of girls who would debate the issues of the day over breakfast at the cafeteria. The group got so involved in their discussions that they frequently lost track of time and had to race off to class lest they be late.

Although some of her classmates prided themselves on their clothes and fashion sense, Hillary was still utterly unconcerned with her own looks. "Hillary hid herself in shapeless denim dresses or sweater-vests over awning-striped bell-bottoms," writes Gail Sheehy. "Her long blond hair was dimming into a mousy brown but she paid no attention, pulling it back with a rubber band or twisting it up into a careless bun."[20] No makeup and a pair of thick eyeglasses with a heavy black frame completed her look. Although she lived and studied among women who prided themselves on wearing the very latest fashions from New York and Paris,

Hillary refused to compete with them. Toward the end of her freshman year she began to date a young man who was a junior at nearby Harvard University, but their dates together were more about debating politics and issues with groups of friends than they were about romance.

Hillary's letters from her first years away from home reveal a bright, sensitive young woman who was trying to find herself. She wrote long letters to Reverend Don Jones, her former mentor in Park Ridge, about searching for her own identity and wondering what kind of person she would become. "I wonder who is me," Hillary once told a friend. "I wonder if I'll ever meet her. If I did, I think we'd get along famously."[21]

DR. MARTIN LUTHER KING'S ASSASSINATION

During a visit home to Park Ridge the summer after her freshman year at Wellesley, Hillary visited Chicago and saw the aftermath of violent race riots that had shaken the city. Streets were littered with debris, windows were broken, and there was a strong police presence in the neighborhoods that she had once visited with her University of Life group. The experience shook Hillary, and she began to make an emotional connection with the issues that she had been debating all year from the safe, peaceful confines of Wellesley.

Two years later, in the spring of her junior year, Hillary's world was shaken profoundly. On April 4, 1968, Dr. Martin

Luther King Jr., the civil rights leader whom Hillary had met years earlier as a high school student, was assassinated in Memphis, Tennessee. Hillary screamed and cried in anger and pain over the news, a profound emotional response from a girl who was thought to be emotionally cold and distant.

Dr. King's assassination had a similar effect on Hillary's classmates, and it drew the sheltered women of Wellesley out into the community at large. Hillary joined several of her friends in donning black arm bands and joining a protest march in Boston. "[We] went into Boston to march in anger and pain,"[22] she later said to a group of students. The assassination had brought the issue of civil rights to a head, and the Wellesley students were no longer willing to amiably discuss their concerns with the administration. The students protested on campus that the Wellesley administration did not appear to be sensitive enough to race relations or diversifying the student body by bringing in more students of color.

BRINGING ABOUT CHANGE

College students all over the country were taking up arms against "The Establishment," as the people in charge were called, and they railed against the government and its policies, threatening to tear down or burn the very colleges that educated them. Hillary found herself at the center of Wellesley's protests, but she never engaged in the inflammatory rhetoric of some student leaders.

HILLARY'S PARENTS MISSED HER GRADUATION

Hugh and Dorothy Rodham were curiously absent from Hillary's shining moment at Wellesley College, when she spoke at graduation. Author Gail Sheehy explored the situation in her book, Hillary's Choice:

"It should have been the peak of pride for her father. But Hillary's father was competitive with his gifted daughter. Hugh Rodham had always held the bar of achievement higher than she could reach. . . . On this day, when his daughter was being graduated from one of the top colleges in the country and making national history as the only student commencement speaker Wellesley had ever had, Hugh Rodham was not there. For reasons never explained, neither Hugh nor Dorothy nor her brothers went to Hillary's college graduation."

Hillary's way was always to work from within, communicating with the campus administration rather than against it to achieve the changes that she sought.

In other words Hillary had chosen to employ politics to seek change. She was beginning to define her own belief in politics, which had less to do with campaigning and swaying voters' minds and more to do with effecting positive changes in society. As she would say upon graduating the following year, "The challenge now is to practice politics as the art of making what appears to be impossible, possible."[23] At the end of her junior year she campaigned for and won the presidency of the student body. From that position, she reasoned, she could spend her senior year working for change with the administration of Wellesley while being an advocate for the entire student body.

In the summer of 1968, before her senior year at Wellesley began, Hillary went to Washington, D.C., to work as an intern for Republican congressman Harold Collier. It was her first extended period in the nation's capital, the site of so many of Hillary's future successes and failures, and she embraced it. She loved the nonstop political debates and the challenge of working for change through government. Her job was to research and write papers on issues like how the government was financing the ongoing war in Vietnam. In her brief tenure in Washington, she made a strong impression with some of the politicians with whom she interacted. "She presented her viewpoints very forcibly, always had ideas, always defended what she had in mind,"[24] said Melvin Laird, a Republican congressman who worked with Hillary.

At the end of the summer Hillary and a friend from Park Ridge took the train into Chicago to attend the Democratic National Convention. Hundreds of college students from around the country had arrived to protest the war in Vietnam. The Chicago police were charged with keeping the streets orderly and quiet, and as the nation watched on television, the two sides clashed. Hillary and her friend watched with horror as college students their own age were violently beaten by Chicago policemen and dragged off to jail for protesting. Once again, Hillary was shaken to see what could happen when people abandoned political solutions.

A Recognized Student Leader

When Hillary returned to Wellesley that fall to begin her senior year, the campus climate had changed dramatically. All over America student leaders were taking up the call for reform, and this time Wellesley was part of the action. Students at the college demanded that they be treated more as adults, and they forced the administration to make changes in several long-standing campus policies. The students wanted to have more of a voice in how campus events were planned and conducted. In one example Hillary led a

Protesters of the Vietnam War clash with Chicago police during the 1968 Democratic National Convention. This brutal display of police force shocked and horrified Hillary Rodham.

HILLARY RECALLS HER COLLEGE YEARS

As reported in Donnie Radcliffe's biography, Hillary Rodham Clinton: A First Lady for Our Time, *Hillary remembers her law school years at Yale as being a powerful era when students questioned everything about society:*

"There was a lot of confusion in our minds. Many arguments took place over food and drink and books in and out of the halls of the law school over what direction our country was heading. A lot of passion, a lot of concern. And what I remember most during that time is the seriousness with which all of us . . . took the challenges that confronted our country."

group that lobbied the administration to allow a student to speak at graduation ceremonies. This had never happened at Wellesley, and the administration was reluctant to change the tradition. Finally, just days before Hillary's class was to graduate, the administration relented. The students and administration agreed that Hillary would be the first student commencement speaker in Wellesley's history.

The featured speaker that day was Senator Edward Burke of Massachusetts, the same senator whom Hillary had helped get elected three years earlier. He gave what many considered to be a standard graduation speech that urged the students to go out and support their government. In a move that shocked many of the people in attendance, Hillary amended her prepared remarks to rebut his speech and challenge leaders like Burke to be more sensitive to her generation. "We are, all of us, exploring a world that none of us understands, and attempting to create within that uncertainty," she declared.

"We're searching for more immediate, ecstatic . . . modes of living."[25] Her fellow graduates leaped to their feet and gave Hillary a seven-minute standing ovation. That summer, *Life* magazine named her as one of the best and brightest student leaders in the nation.

But where to go from Wellesley? Hillary had had a taste of politics and government, and she liked it. Many of her classmates would choose a more traditional path of marrying young and becoming stay-at-home mothers. Hillary wanted more. She decided that she could continue her interests in effecting positive changes in society by receiving a legal education. Becoming a lawyer would allow her to seek any number of jobs in Washington policy-making circles and would be a good background if she decided to run for political office one day. Her grades and record of service qualified her to be admitted into any law school in the country, but she narrowed her choices to Harvard and Yale Universities. Each school is distinguished and known for its rigorous law programs. Her decision was made when she met a law professor from Harvard at a party who pompously announced that "we don't need any more women [in our program]."[26] She made plans to attend Yale University Law School in New Haven, Connecticut, in the fall of 1969.

HILLARY BECOMES A RISING STAR AT YALE

Hillary was one of only thirty women to enter Yale's law school in the fall of 1969, but she immediately distinguished herself on campus. By the second semester of her first year, writes Donnie Radcliffe, Hillary "was a woman to watch at Yale. In the law school dining hall, as she had [been] at Wellesley, she was the magnet."[27] Hillary found herself entering into the spirited, open debate between students and the Yale administration about politics, society, and how the university should be operated. During one heated debate between students about a civil rights issue, Hillary sat on a table and calmly mediated the discussion, keeping the participants from sinking into a shouting match. Hillary "was passionately antiwar, antibusiness and suspicious of the police and was beginning to think about women's and environmental issues," writes author Joyce Milton. "What set her apart from the true radicals was that she had little faith in direct action. She wanted to keep lines of communication to the administration open and work through existing institutions."[28]

It was at that time that Hillary met Marian Wright Edelman, a graduate of Yale Law School who was doing pioneering legal and social work on behalf of underprivileged children. It was a subject that had long interested Hillary, and she asked Edelman if she could work with her that summer. Edelman had received national recognition for being the first black woman to pass the bar exam in Mississippi and for creating the Children's Defense Fund, which was one of the first advocacy groups created to look out for the needs of children. The older woman said that she would welcome the help but that there was no money to pay for Hillary's time. Undeterred, Hillary combed through library books and government publications and won a grant that would allow her to work for the Children's Defense Fund that summer. It was the beginning of a long professional and personal relationship that influenced Hillary deeply. "In one of those strange twists of fate that enters all our lives if we're open to hear and to see them, I knew right away that I had to go to work for her,"[29] she later said.

In the summer of 1970 Hillary went to work in Washington on behalf of the Children's Defense Fund. Her job was to study migratory labor, and she spent much of the summer traveling around the country to interview migrant workers. She asked them about how their children lived, how the children spent their days when the parents were working in the fields, and how the children's needs were met. She saw that many of the children were receiving no education or health care, and she reported her findings back to Washington, D.C., where the Children's Defense Fund could use the information to lobby Congress for funding on behalf of the children.

The experience set Hillary on a career path that would influence much of her later life in politics. She resolved to work on behalf of children by becoming an advocate for adequate protection and services for children. Returning to Yale for her second year of law school, she arranged her schedule to allow time to study and work with the Yale Child Study Center, a research organization

Children's rights activist Marian Wright Edelman became a friend and mentor to Hillary Rodham.

that focused on children. She spent long hours studying issues that affected children and learning about child abuse, which in the 1960s was just being identified as a serious issue for children's health and well-being.

HILLARY MEETS BILL CLINTON

Hillary had had several boyfriends up to that time, but none of the relationships had been serious. All that was about to change. At the law library one night, Hillary was studying hard, buried in books as usual, when she noticed a young man watching her intently from across the room. His name was Bill Clinton, and he was a first-year law student from Arkansas who intended to pursue a career in politics as soon as he graduated from law school.

Hillary and Bill had one class together but were not acquainted. At the library Hillary decided to take the initiative. She walked over to Clinton, who was still staring at her and said, "Look, you've been staring at me for five minutes. The least you can do is introduce yourself."[30] Clinton was smitten, and so was Hillary. Their romance began immediately.

Hillary Rodham and Bill Clinton seemed to complement each other perfectly. They both loved to talk and argue politics, and they both had brilliant, lively intellects. Bill was handsome and engaging. He pretended to be a down-home southern boy by reciting statistics about the number of watermelons grown in his

"An Oversize Teddy Bear"

Hillary and Bill seemed to be made for each other. "It was love at first sight" on Hillary's part, reports author Joyce Milton in The First Partner: Hillary Rodham Clinton, *as she characterizes the young man who stole Hillary's heart:*

"Tall and stocky, Clinton, when not working on a campaign, hid his boyish features behind a beard, which gave him the look of an oversize teddy bear. And, of course, he was ambitious, almost as much so as Hillary. . . . His culinary skills were limited to slapping together peanut-butter sandwiches. Clinton had trouble getting places on time and could be flummoxed (exasperated) by simple errands. He missed a lot of classes doing political work . . . and stayed up half the night reading books that had nothing to do with his schoolwork. . . . Clinton had that slow drawl and the Southerner's sense that sometimes the good things in life can come easily—a revelation to Hillary, who had internalized the Rodham belief in hard work and struggle."

home state, but behind the country bumpkin façade was a sharp and agile mind that could absorb and digest reams of information.

The couple began to live together in a three-room apartment. They hosted friends for memorable evenings of eating dinner, drinking wine, and passionately discussing politics and the events of the day. That winter Bill visited Hillary at her parents' home in Park Ridge. He impressed Hugh and Dorothy with his eloquence and charm, but not his politics. Hillary's new love was a Democrat.

Hillary's politics were evolving at that time, too. She had become increasingly disenchanted with the Republican Party during her college years and did not support the current Republican president,

Richard M. Nixon. As the Republican Party grew more conservative during the Nixon administration, she found herself pulled farther away from it. Hillary began to look for candidates from either party who reflected her views against the war and for the rights of children and women.

The candidate that she supported that year was George McGovern, the senator from South Dakota who opposed Nixon's reelection. Along with Bill, Hillary went to Texas in the summer of 1972 in support of McGovern. McGovern's main attraction to many voters, including Hillary, was that he advocated ending the Vietnam War. She and Bill stayed with the campaign until that fall, working long hours to try to rally support for McGovern. Their efforts failed, and they returned to Yale when Nixon defeated McGovern and began his second term.

LIFE AFTER LAW SCHOOL

Hillary graduated from law school in the spring of 1972, but she chose to remain at Yale for an extra year, mainly to stay close to Bill. She used her time to study child development issues and assist the Yale New Haven Hospital with creating legal policies to deal with the issue of child abuse.

When Bill graduated in the spring of 1973, the couple had a difficult decision to make. Bill's overriding ambition was to return to Arkansas to begin his political career; he had been focused on winning elective office in his home state since his high school years. Hillary's choice was not as clear. She could not picture herself being a politician's wife in Arkansas, but her attraction and love for Bill were undeniable.

The couple decided to try to continue to see each other while working and living in different states. Bill got a job teaching law at the University of Arkansas, and Hillary accepted a staff position in Washington, D.C., with Marion Wright Edelman's Children's Defense Fund. Much of her job involved traveling across the country to interview school officials and compare census figures with school enrollments. She was shocked to learn that there were thousands of school-aged children across America who were not in school and that no government agency was trying to correct this problem.

"We found children who were being kept out of school because they had mental or physical problems," Hillary later said. "Or we'd find children whose families were new immigrants and were afraid to send them to school. We'd find children who were too poor. I traveled to different states and was involved in lawsuits about juvenile issues. That's what I cared about, what I wanted to do."[31]

HILLARY WORKS TO IMPEACH PRESIDENT NIXON

Her mission was interrupted at the beginning of 1974 when twenty-six-year-old Hillary was asked to join an inquiry into the growing Watergate scandal that had begun during the previous presidential campaign. The evidence was mounting that President Nixon and his staff had tampered with the campaign in any number of ways, from stealing documents at the Watergate building in Washington, D.C., to conducting "dirty tricks" to discredit Democratic candidates. The House of Representatives demanded that an independent investigation be undertaken.

The head of the investigative committee, John Doar, had met and been impressed with Hillary as a student at Yale. He picked her to be one of forty-three lawyers, only three of whom were women, to conduct the investigation.

In Washington's superheated political climate, the Republicans accused Democrats of making up the charges against Nixon. The Democrats were furious that the presidential election had been tampered with and accused the Republicans of trying to hide serious, and criminal, offenses. In this atmosphere Hillary's legal team had to make absolutely certain that they got their information right and presented it in a clear way that would not suggest partisan politics at work. Any mistakes they made would be viciously attacked and criticized by one side or the other.

The team worked tirelessly to investigate the many facets of the Watergate scandal. Working eighteen-hour days, they interviewed hundreds of people and studied reams of documents that related to the case, many of which implicated high-ranking officials on the president's staff, as well as Nixon himself. Hillary spent much of her time listening to White House tapes of conversations between the president and his closest advisers. "I was kind of locked in this soundproof room with these big headphones on, listening to a tape," she later recalled. "It was surreal, unbelievable, but it was a real positive experience because the system worked. It was done in a very professional, careful way."[32]

Hillary works with the House Impeachment Committee to investigate President Nixon's role in the Watergate scandal.

Bill Clinton and Hillary Rodham pose for a portrait. In 1974 Hillary made the decision to follow Bill to Arkansas.

By the end of June 1974, the team had finished their investigation. Their findings were put into thirty-six large, black binders, a staggering amount of evidence that proved that President Nixon and his circle of advisers had engineered the Watergate break-in and other illegal acts during the campaign. A month later the House Judiciary Committee, which had been empowered by the House of Representatives to investigate the case, voted to impeach the president. A few weeks after that, on August 9, 1974, President Nixon resigned. It was the only time in history that an American president has resigned his office.

Her job finished, Hillary had a difficult decision to make. She was suddenly out of a job and finished with law school. She could have returned to the Children's Defense Fund or gotten a position with any number of high-powered law firms in Washington, D.C., or Chicago. But Hillary's heart belonged in Arkansas, where Bill Clinton continued to live and teach and prepare for his first run at political office. In her mind, Arkansas was far removed from the action that had so stimulated her since she had left home in Park Ridge and embarked on her education at Wellesley and Yale. Issues of feminism and the rights of women were sweeping the nation, and Hillary had to decide whether she wanted to choose love and marriage or a high-powered career and the kind of political influence that she was developing as a Washington insider.

Hillary chose to listen to her heart. "Much as I would have liked to deny it," she said later, "there was something very special about Bill and there was something very important between us."[33] As her friends and colleagues on the impeachment committee went off to pursue their legal careers in New York, Washington, D.C., and San Francisco, Hillary packed her things and headed south to Arkansas. The passionate defender of children, bright legal mind, and debater of issues would soon take on a new role: the wife of a political candidate.

Chapter

3 Northern Style Meets Southern Politics

My friends and family thought I had lost my mind. I was a little bit concerned about that as well.

—Hillary, on moving to Arkansas to be with Bill

When Hillary arrived in Fayetteville, Arkansas, in September 1974, there was a rally in the city for the university's beloved football team, the University of Arkansas Razorbacks. A razorback is a kind of pig, and people had dressed up in pig noses and hats and were running through the streets screaming, "Sou-eee, sou-eee, pig, pig, pig!"[34] This was the greeting that the serious-minded young lawyer from Yale University and the House Impeachment Committee received on her arrival to her new home.

Hillary had been offered a job to teach at the university's law school, where she would teach classes in criminal law and criminal procedure. Bill Clinton was also teaching at the law school, but his energies were more directed to his first political campaign. He was running for a seat in the U.S. House of Representatives, and Hillary immediately went to work in his cluttered campaign headquarters. She organized the office and began to help him plan his strategy and campaign. It was a role that she would play many times.

HILLARY MAKES A DIFFERENCE

Hillary was all business in the classroom. She quickly developed a reputation for being a tough teacher who demanded excellence from her students and did not give high grades easily. She was not content just to collect her paycheck as a professor of law, however. Her commitment to politics and service that had begun at Wellesley was as strong as ever. She was surprised to see that very few women were working as lawyers in Arkansas, and she lobbied the administration of the university to hire more women. She also saw a need for low-income people, and even criminals in jail, to have a way to receive legal assistance even if they could not pay for it. Many low-income people could not afford to hire a lawyer to represent them, so she began a program that used the students and faculty of the law school to provide legal assistance to people who could not afford it. She and her students prepared legal papers and represented everyone from convicted criminals seeking parole to low-income people who wanted to file for divorce. In its first year the clinic advised three hundred clients and took fifty cases to court. She also worked with women in the community to establish the first clinic for rape victims in Fayetteville.

Hillary quickly grew comfortable in Fayetteville. She found the town to be friendly and accepting of her. "I liked people tapping me on the shoulder at the grocery store and saying, 'Aren't you that lady professor at the law school?'" she said. "It was an adjustment in the sense that I'd never really lived in the South and I'd never lived in a small town, but I felt so immediately at home."[35]

Hillary and Bill were becoming known in the community as a fun couple who also liked to get things done. It would have seemed scandalous at the time in Arkansas for the unwed couple to live together. They kept separate apartments but spent most of their free time together. They were known for giving lively dinner parties that nearly always wound up

Hillary Rodham (left) looks on as Bill Clinton begins his campaign to win a seat in the House of Representatives. Hillary played a large role in managing this campaign.

"THE FEAT OF A SUPERWOMAN"

In Hillary's Choice *author Gail Sheehy admires Hillary's ability to work on important federal commissions in Washington, D.C., while continuing to live and work in Little Rock:*

"She was an indefatigable networker. Through her activism with the CDF (Children's Defense Fund), the LSC (Legal Services Corporation), and the ABA (American Bar Association), Hillary kept in close contact with her East Coast colleagues from Wellesley, Yale, and the Watergate committee. It was truly the feat of a superwoman to forge all these activist links around the country from a remote home base in Arkansas and to direct the efforts of LSC's five thousand lawyers spread across 335 legal services offices and handling a million cases a year—all the while continuing to practice law at the Rose firm."

with a spirited game of charades. On weekends they played volleyball with friends.

After a year Hillary still was not sure that she wanted to commit herself to living and working in Arkansas. During a summer vacation she visited her friends and family in order to evaluate her direction in life. She wanted to see if she had made the right decision in moving to Arkansas. She visited friends in Park Ridge, Wellesley, Boston, New York, and Washington, D.C., where she had long conversations about work, politics, feminism, and the opportunities to be of service to the community. "I didn't see anything out there that I thought was more exciting or challenging than what I had in front of me,"[36] she said. She returned to Fayetteville refreshed and ready to continue her work.

HILLARY MARRIES WILLIAM JEFFERSON CLINTON

Bill had a surprise waiting for her. He, too, had been doing a lot of thinking, and he had decided to ask Hillary to marry him. He had discussed the matter with his mother, Virginia Kelley, who was not so sure that the educated young woman from Chicago was the right match for her precious eldest son. Bill tried to convince her to accept Hillary as her daughter-in-law. "Mother, pray that it's Hillary," Bill begged her. "Because I'll tell you this: for me, it's Hillary or it's nobody."[37]

Hillary had once commented that she liked a small house that the couple had seen near the campus in Fayetteville. While she was away, Bill bought and decorated the house with an antique bed and flowered sheets. When Hillary returned from her summer vacation, he drove her to the house. "Now you'd better marry me because I can't live there all by myself,"[38] he said. It took the practical, level-headed Hillary two months to agree.

Hillary did not want the wedding to be elaborate. She invited only her family and a few friends to attend the service, which would be held at their new home. There was no engagement ring, and the night before the wedding, Hillary's mother was shocked to find out that her daughter had not even picked out a wedding dress. Hillary was so unaccustomed to thinking about things like clothes or her own personal appearance that she had simply forgotten to buy one. She and Dorothy ran out to a store, and Hillary bought the first bridal gown that fit her.

On Saturday, October 11, 1975, Hillary Diane Rodham and William Jefferson Clinton were married. A reception was held at the home of a friend, where about two hundred friends and family had gathered to dance, listen to music, and toast the new couple with champagne. Instead of a honeymoon the couple went to Mexico for a vacation; they were accompanied by Hillary's parents and brothers.

Hillary had another surprise in store for the polite southern society in general and her proper southern mother-in-law in particular: She decided not to change her name. Hillary continued being known as

Bill Clinton and Hillary share a laugh. The couple married on October 11, 1975.

Hillary Rodham, not Hillary Clinton. It was a decision that would haunt her and Bill in the coming years.

CAMPAIGNING SEPARATELY

Soon after the wedding, the young couple went off to work on two different political campaigns. Bill had decided to run for the position of attorney general of Arkansas; Hillary volunteered to work in the campaign of Jimmy Carter, the governor of Georgia who was running for president of the United States on the Democratic ticket against Republican Gerald Ford.

The coordinators of the Carter campaign asked Hillary to go to Indiana to try to win votes. It was a tough assignment because Indiana had long voted Republican, and securing votes there for the Democrat Carter would not be easy. Hillary plunged into the challenge with her usual enthusiasm. She opened Carter campaign offices in ninety-two counties throughout the state and coordinated volunteers. She quickly became known as a person who could get things done, and she was tenacious at getting people to do things her way.

"She could out-argue anybody," one colleague recalled, "and the last thing you wanted to do, particularly if it was at the end of the day and you were dead tired, was to disagree with her. You always knew she was going to win."[39]

On election day Hillary stayed in Indianapolis and watched the presidential election returns. Jimmy Carter, a plainspoken peanut farmer from Georgia, narrowly won the presidential election. For the first time since 1968, when she first became disenchanted with the Republican Party and began to campaign on behalf of Democratic candidates, Hillary had attained her goal of seeing a Democrat win the presidency.

Bill met success in his campaign, too. Handsome and earnest, he won the election easily and became attorney general of Arkansas. It was his first political victory and set the stage for his bright future in politics.

HILLARY JOINS THE ROSE LAW FIRM

With the campaigns completed, Bill and Hillary moved to Little Rock, the state capital of Arkansas. The wife of a state's attorney general was not expected to have a job of her own, but Hillary was different. She decided to begin practicing law. In February 1977 she accepted a job with the Rose Law Firm, one of the largest firms in Arkansas. There she represented clients in civil and criminal cases, branching out into areas of law that she had never before explored.

Hillary kept a full load of casework at the law firm, but she also used her time to promote some of her personal causes. She began an organization called Arkansas Advocates for Children and Families, a statewide program that provided legal assistance for families who could not otherwise afford to hire lawyers. The group also successfully lobbied the Arkansas

Jimmy Carter talks with a factory worker during his 1976 presidential campaign. With Carter's victory, Hillary achieved her goal of helping to elect a Democratic president.

legislature to set aside funds for new child care programs. In one important case Hillary won the rights for a couple to keep custody of the foster child they had raised for nearly three years. Hillary convinced the judge that the child's best interests lay in staying with the foster parents he had known since infancy, rather than returning to his biological mother who had given him up at birth.

Also that year, as a gesture of thanks for her work during his campaign, President Carter appointed Hillary to head the Legal Services Corporation, a federal program that provided legal assistance to the poor. She was also a board member for the Children's Defense Fund, the child advocacy group for whom she had worked while studying at Yale. Although she still maintained her busy work load in Arkansas, Hillary flew to Washington, D.C., every month for meetings that involved coordinating hundreds of lawyers and caseworkers around the country who offered legal services to the poor in their communities.

THE FIRST LADY OF ARKANSAS

In the meantime Bill Clinton set his sights on becoming the governor of Arkansas. He announced his candidacy in 1978 and used all of the skill and charm he possessed to capture votes. He swept through the primaries as the leading candidate and then crushed his Republican opponent in the general election. At thirty-two years old, he became one of the youngest governors in American history. At the same time Hillary, at thirty-one years old, became the first lady of Arkansas. Unlike her many other roles, this was one for which she was not prepared.

During the late-1970s most first ladies stayed home to raise children and attend to ceremonial duties such as appearing at schools to read to children or holding social functions like teas and dinners at the governor's mansion. Hillary Rodham, however, had a full-time job in a very demanding profession, as well as many outside interests. She even took on important roles in state government. In a move that shocked many traditionalists in Arkansas, Bill named Hillary to head the Rural Health Advisory Committee in 1979, which was established to develop a program of delivering health care to people in isolated communities.

Hillary's businesslike attitude and no-nonsense approach to conducting meetings were a shock to some of the forty-four board members on the committee. "If I were a man," she lamented, "they would probably say what a great, strong person this fellow is, how commanding he is, and all the rest. . . . I'm not reluctant to say what's on my mind, and if some people interpret that one way instead of another, I can't help that."[40]

CHELSEA CLINTON IS BORN

Bill and Hillary were also trying to have a child, and in late 1979, Hillary found out that she was pregnant. She maintained her whirlwind schedule of work and travel right up to the last month of the pregnancy. On February 27, 1980, she gave birth to Chelsea Victoria Clinton, who was named after a popular folk song, "Chelsea Morning," that both of the Clintons enjoyed, as well as a neighborhood in the city of London where they had vacationed that year.

It had been a difficult delivery for Hillary that ended in a Caesarian section, and the Clintons stayed in the hospital for the first three days of Chelsea's life. Bill spent nearly all of his time in the hospital with his wife and new daughter. The Clintons seemed to forget that they were the political leaders of the state. In all of the excitement over their daughter's birth, they forgot to issue a birth announcement or invite the local press in to record the event. Chelsea was not introduced to the public for several days. Many people in Arkansas felt that their governor was ignoring them, and many were outraged that the first lady continued to use her maiden name even after the child was born. It was not a slight that Arkansas voters would easily forget.

Being a mother was an entirely new adventure for Hillary, an adventure for which all of her education and political awareness had not prepared her. Initially she took four months off work from the law firm to care for Chelsea, although Hillary continued to attend monthly meetings of the Legal Services Corporation in Washington, D.C., with Chelsea in tow and Bill along to help her care for the baby. Like any new mother, Hillary had to learn how to adjust to the baby's needs. At one point, when Chelsea was crying nonstop despite Hillary's efforts to soothe her, Hillary said, "Chelsea, we're in this together. You've never been a baby before and I've never been a mother before.

We're going to help each other understand all this."[41]

Hillary enjoyed her new role so much that she extended her leave, working only part time at the law office through the summer of 1980. This time with Chelsea reinforced Hillary's beliefs about the importance of parents being able to care for their newborn infants without fear of losing their jobs or health benefits.

REELECTION TROUBLE

At the same time Bill's campaign to be reelected to a second term as governor

Hillary poses with her husband in front of the Arkansas governor's mansion. In 1978 Bill became the youngest governor in the state's history.

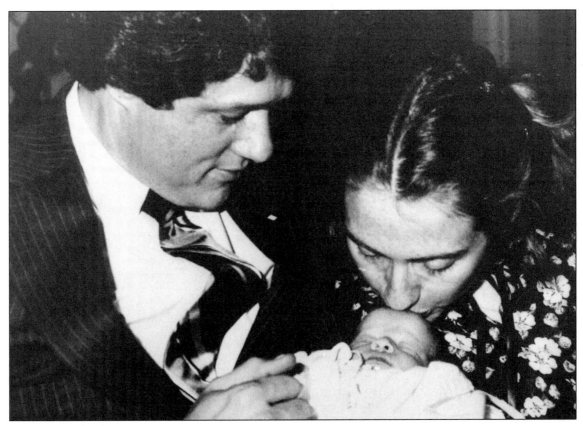

Hillary kisses Chelsea. She loved being a new mother so much that she extended her maternity leave from the Rose Law Firm.

was showing signs of weakness. He found his popularity slipping among Arkansas voters. Many observers felt that he had been too distracted by the birth of his daughter. Also many people in Arkansas felt that the young governor had surrounded himself with people who did not understand the needs or problems of his state. Many of his staff members were young intellectuals with very liberal views.

The resentment of Arkansas residents turned on Hillary, the first lady who was so different from traditional southern wives. Wrote Gail Sheehy,

To southerners expecting a more decorative First Lady, Hillary Rodham was almost an eyesore. She rejected makeup, glared through thick glasses, drowned herself in big, shapeless fishermans' sweaters and bell-bottoms, and adamantly stuck to her maiden name.[42]

The resentment added up. In the general election of 1980 Bill was defeated by his Republican opponent, a Little Rock businessman named Frank White. Bill was crushed. He had not expected to lose, and his political aspirations were suspended indefinitely. "Bill Clinton was an instant has-been," wrote a *Time* magazine reporter. "The main reason: voters had been alienated by Clinton's hifalutin ambitions."[43]

Hillary was also disappointed by Bill's defeat. Many of her friends wondered if she could continue to live in Arkansas when her husband was no longer a major political figure. Hillary responded to the setback by working harder. She went back to work at the Rose Law Firm and continued to flourish. She took on more cases and began to make a name for herself as a strong advocate for her clients. She had the legal skills and persuasive talents to win decisions in the courtroom. She kept a very busy schedule but always found time for Chelsea and Bill. She made sure that she was with Chelsea at the beginning and end of every day. "The most important thing in my life is my family—my daughter and my husband, particularly my daughter because I think you have to put children first,"[44] Hillary told a reporter.

On Chelsea's second birthday Bill announced that he would run again for governor in 1982. This time Hillary would do whatever it took to get her husband back into office. She legally changed her name to Hillary Rodham Clinton. "It was not a decision that was easy to make for me, but it was one that I made, thinking it was the best for me and the best for my husband,"[45] she later said. That spring she also got rid of her heavy eyeglasses, replacing them with contact lenses, and had her hair restyled.

Hillary was Bill's chief adviser, helping to plan every appearance and aspect of the campaign as he traveled throughout the state in search of votes. "This is a very personal state that requires a high level of accessibility," said Bill. "I'm ready to correct past mistakes."[46] Once again, the people of Arkansas embraced him.

In January 1983 Bill Clinton was inaugurated as governor of Arkansas for the second time. Hillary was thrilled to return to the arena of politics and policy making. The family moved back into the governor's mansion. The Clintons would remain in the governor's mansion for the next ten years.

HILLARY TACKLES EDUCATION REFORM

Shortly after taking office for the second time, Bill Clinton saw a serious problem in his home state. Arkansas had a terrible educational system that ranked among the worst in the country. Not only were many teenagers failing to complete their high school educations, dropping out of school early and giving up the idea of college educations entirely, but students across the state were producing some of the worst standardized test scores in the nation. Schools were underfunded and in need of repairs, and class sizes were getting too large. Most alarming was a prevailing mentality among many Arkansans that their children just did not have what it takes to be good students.

When they studied the problem, Bill and Hillary concluded that the only thing that could revitalize education in Arkansas was to completely overhaul the system. This would be an enormous political undertaking that would require the cooperation of the state's politicians, many of whom had to be convinced that there was a problem in the first place, as well as the teachers and school districts and the citizens of the state, who would be asked to pay more taxes to improve education.

To work on the problem, Bill created the Education Standards Committee to investigate ways of improving and changing the state's educational system. He named Hillary to be in charge of the committee. Some critics howled that he was not serious about the problem if he named his own wife to be in charge of the solution or that he was handing out plum jobs in his administration to his family. But Hillary brushed off the criticism and began to tackle the new challenge with her usual tenacity.

Hillary remembered well that her own parents, Hugh and Dorothy, had made sure during her childhood that school was her priority, and that she had grown up with the advantage of a strong school system in Illinois. To begin her campaign to bring Arkansas up to the same level, she traveled throughout the state, visiting each one of the 371 school districts, meeting people, and asking for suggestions on how they would improve the system. She also began to make strong speeches and public statements that challenged Arkansas to raise the level of education. "One of the principal problems we face in our state, and apparently in the country, is that we are not expecting enough of ourselves, our schools, or our students,"[47] she said. Hillary encouraged schools to give students the same respect for bringing home good grades as they would for students who were good athletes.

STARTING EDUCATION EARLY

Hillary was particularly proud of HIPPY, the Home Instruction Program for Preschool Youngsters that she helped start in Arkansas, because it brought education for children into the home at an early age, as she pointed out in The Unique Voice of Hillary Rodham Clinton:

"It became clear to me that we could have the most astonishing schools in the world and we would still not be reaching the needs of all of our children, because half of all learning occurs by the time a person is five. And the way that our children are treated in the first five years—the way their health is attended to, to say nothing of intellectual stimulation and family support—will have a very big influence on how well they can do for the rest of their lives."

Hillary Rodham Clinton speaks at an Educational Standards Commission meeting in 1983. Her work on that committee brought many improvements to Arkansas's public school system.

She also focused her attention on the teachers and administrators. "Quit making excuses [about the poor quality of education in the state]," she demanded in a speech, adding that a school "that passes illiterate and semi-literate students commits educational fraud."[48] A key component of the plan that the committee developed was that teachers would have to undergo testing to prove that they were competent to teach students. It was an idea that shocked the educational establishment and enraged teachers who felt that they did not have to prove anything. They protested the testing component, but Hillary stuck to it.

After four months of research she brought her proposal to the state legislature for approval. She gave an impassioned speech to the legislators about the need to change the educational system, and she outlined, point by point, her ideas for making it better and for earning their support in the form of allocating more tax dollars to education. The plan passed, new taxes were raised, and when the teachers had their first competency test, 10 percent of them failed it and were removed from their classrooms.

At the same time that she was tackling educational reform, Hillary saw a need for more Arkansas parents to learn how to prepare their children at a young age for education. Many parents did not know that reading to a child was crucial to the child's future success in school. Hillary introduced a program called the Home Instruction Program for Preschool Youngsters (nicknamed "HIPPY"), which sent teachers into the homes of underprivileged families to help train parents how to better prepare their children for school.

Hillary liked the role of working for change within Bill's administration. It fit her concept of using politics as a way of helping people improve their lives. For her efforts Hillary was named the Arkansas Woman of the Year in 1983 and the state's Young Mother of the Year in 1984. She realized that she could help change things in society for the better while still supporting Bill's political ambitions in Arkansas. She herself was not interested in running for elective office, and she saw that much could be accomplished as the governor's wife. "I just knew I wanted to be part of changing the world," she would later tell a reporter. "Bill's desire to be in public life was much more specific than my desire to do good."[49]

BILL DECIDES TO RUN FOR PRESIDENT

With Bill running for reelection and winning four straight times, the Clintons continued to live in the governor's mansion in Little Rock throughout the 1980s. Hillary not only became a recognized lawyer—she was named one of America's 100 Most Powerful Lawyers in 1988 and 1991—but she served on corporate boards

and continued to champion causes on behalf of the health and education of children. She also served as chairperson of the Children's Defense Fund, for which she had been doing work ever since her college days at Yale.

Hillary was also the family's principal breadwinner. As governor, Bill made a modest salary of $35,000 a year, but Hillary brought home as much as $175,000. She made astute investments that brought in more money for the family, but the Clintons did not show off their wealth. Hillary continued to drive Chelsea to school every morning and she often surprised visitors by opening the door to the governor's mansion wearing blue jeans.

At the same time, Bill was making a name for himself as a governor who had higher political aspirations, and he had the combination of charisma, brains, and political know-how to win a national election. He thought about running for president in 1988 but decided to stay out of the race. "Our daughter is seven," he explained to a crowd of supporters about his decision not to run. "She is the most important person in the world to us and our most important responsibility. In order to wage a winning campaign, both Hillary and I would have to leave her for long periods of time. That would not be good for her or for us."[50]

In the summer of 1991 President George Bush's ratings had begun to slip, and the national economy was at a low point. Bill saw that his opportunity to run for president had come. He and Hillary discussed the matter long and

Bill and Chelsea Clinton leave an Arkansas voting booth in 1986. Because of Chelsea's age, her parents decided to postpone Bill's presidential bid until 1992.

TAKING ON ALL CHALLENGERS

Hillary was an outspoken advocate for Bill during all of his campaigns to be reelected as governor of Arkansas. In Hillary Rodham Clinton: A First Lady for Our Time *author Donnie Radcliffe offers a vivid example of how Hillary would fearlessly take on her husband's political opponents:*

"Accustomed by now to speaking her mind, Hillary dropped by a photo op . . . to take on a Democrat who wanted her husband's job. Challenger Tom McRae hadn't expected the First Lady of Arkansas as a stand-in when he called a press conference to accuse Clinton of being too pigeon-hearted to debate him on the issues. Yet, sure enough, there stood Hillary demanding to know: 'Do you really want an answer, Tom? Do you really want a response from Bill when you know he's in Washington doing work for the state? That sounds a bit like a stunt to me.'"

hard, considering how a win or a loss would affect Bill, Hillary, Chelsea, and their home state of Arkansas. In October 1991 Bill formally announced his intention to run for the Democratic nomination in the 1992 election. His theme was contained in a single, powerful word: change.

4 The Two-for-One Presidency

When you think of Hillary, think of our real slogan: Buy one, get one free!
—Bill Clinton, during the 1992 presidential campaign

The Clintons knew that together they formed a powerful political team. Hillary had worked closely with Bill during all of his reelection campaigns in Arkansas, and they saw no reason why she should not be just as involved with the presidential campaign of 1992. Bill saw Hillary's sharp legal mind and decisiveness as an asset, and he was proud of her ability to communicate with the public and with his closest advisers. He wanted to show the American people that Hillary would make a fine first lady. Because of her education, career, and public advocacy, she would be more involved in the running of the government than any first lady had ever been.

Neither he nor Hillary realized the backlash that would be felt by Americans who were not ready for a first lady like Hillary. As the Clintons would quickly learn, the idea of a "two-for-one presidency" was not embraced by many voters.

HILLARY'S ROLE IN THE CAMPAIGN

There had been charismatic and outspoken first ladies in the past, such as Eleanor Roosevelt, Betty Ford, and Rosalynn Carter. But no first lady or candidate's wife had ever been so visible, so prominent, or so very clearly a part of the inner workings of a campaign as Hillary was during the presidential campaign of 1992. As one *Vanity Fair* magazine writer reported during the campaign, "It is Hillary Rodham Clinton . . . who is the diesel engine powering the front-running Democratic campaign."[51]

Hillary gave speeches during the campaign on behalf of Bill's candidacy in which she would occasionally lapse from saying what "my husband" would accomplish to the simpler "we." She raised funds for the campaign, going to Hollywood to speak at fund-raisers among the rich writers and producers whom she had befriended. She even frequently criticized incumbent President George Bush, Clinton's opponent, in speeches. "When it's all stripped away, at bottom what we see is a failure of leadership, rooted in a very hollow sense of what politics is and can be,"[52] she said.

Hillary was also instrumental in setting campaign strategy in Bill's inner circle of advisers. Her most important influence was behind the scenes, where she helped direct the campaign. As *Time* magazine reported during the campaign, "She did not wield power for its own sake, but rather intervened as needed, fixing speeches, poking holes in arguments, warning the Governor of his foes and rewarding his friends. She was the candidate's most pointed critic, arguing

Bill Clinton addresses supporters after winning the 1992 Democratic presidential nomination. Hillary Rodham Clinton played an instrumental role in helping her husband win the nomination.

that he was too passive in the first debate in New Hampshire (he has never been so laid back again), and his most trusted ally. She was much more likely to end a meeting than hold one, the one person who could cut off debate and force a decision."[53]

UNEASINESS OVER HILLARY

Hillary's role quickly became the subject of controversy. The press reported that voters questioned the nature of the "two-for-one presidency," as Bill had jokingly called it. In another first for a candidate's wife, Hillary's every comment was dissected and criticized. Polls were taken to see how the American public viewed her and perceived their marriage. She was called "intense" and "tough-minded," and people questioned the nature of her marriage to Bill, wondering if it was more of a "professional arrangement" than a "real marriage."[54] When the Clintons sat down for a crucial television interview to fight a rumor about Bill's infidelity—a potential scandal that could have killed his campaign early—Hillary won over some people and alienated others by saying, "You know, I'm not sitting here as some little woman standing by my man, like Tammy Wynette."[55]

That comment and another about how she was not the kind of mother who stayed home to bake cookies infuriated and offended a large segment of the population who indeed thought that those were precisely the things a wife and mother should do.

Hillary tried to explain that she didn't expect every woman to follow her path. "Our lives are a mixture of different roles," she observed. "Most of us are doing the best we can to find whatever the right balance is. . . . For me, that balance is family, work and service."[56]

During the general election campaign, the Republicans criticized Hillary, portraying her as a power-crazed, ultrafeminist who was trying to steal the presidency without winning a single vote for herself. Polls showed, however, that every time somebody attacked Hillary, her acceptance by the overall public went up. As James Carville, Clinton's top campaign strategist, pointed out, "The Republican Party in Houston made a collective fool of itself in attacking Hillary. People want to hear other things in an election campaign."[57]

During the last days of the election, the Clintons raced around the country delivering their message of a better economy, a better education, and a sweeping out of the old. They flew back to Little Rock to be home for election night, and on November 3, 1992, Bill Clinton received the votes of 44,908,233 Americans and won the election easily to become the forty-second president of the United States of America.

WHAT ROLE FOR HILLARY?

The Clintons, with twelve-year-old Chelsea in tow, left their home in Arkansas in January 1993 and prepared to move into the White House. With the harsh campaign over, they were greeted warmly by President and Mrs. Bush and made a smooth transition into what would be their home for the next eight years. On the night of January 21, after Bill had been sworn into office with Hillary standing proudly by his side, the couple made the rounds of a dozen different inaugural balls around the city. Hillary wore a stunning sequined outfit, and Bill, in his tuxedo, charmed the crowds by playing a saxophone. The couple danced together and looked every part the successful, young duo that was on top of the world.

But what role would Hillary play in the White House now that her husband had attained the ultimate political prize? Hillary wanted to be involved in making public policy. Many people felt that her lifetime of service had prepared her for a key job in the Clinton administration. Hillary had qualifications that no first lady

in history had ever possessed. "There have been accomplished women in the East Wing," wrote a *Time* magazine reporter, "but there has never been one who would qualify to be White House counsel, if only her husband were not President."[58]

Hillary and Bill were cautious about choosing a role for her in the new administration. They knew that she would be involved in ways that were unprecedented for a first lady, but they realized that many Americans were suspicious about handing over governmental power to Hillary. During the campaign neither she nor Bill would comment specifically on what lay ahead for Hillary if she became first lady. "I want maneuverability," Hillary offered. "I want to get deeply involved in solving problems."[59]

Hillary's influence and strong will were quickly revealed in Washington. Several of her close friends and associates from the

Bill and Hillary dance together at one of the many balls the couple attended following Bill's inauguration.

Rose Law Firm and Children's Defense Fund received important jobs in the Clinton administration thanks to Hillary's recommendations. Bernard Nussbaum, an old friend of Hillary's and her former boss, became White House counsel, and his assistant was Vince Foster, one of Hillary's closest friends and associates in Arkansas. Her boss from the Rose Law Firm, Webster Hubbell, was named associate attorney general, and Donna Shalala, with whom Hillary had served on the CDF board, was named secretary of Health and Human Services.

In one of her first moves as first lady, Hillary banished all smoking from the White House, a move that infuriated supporters of the powerful tobacco industry. Hillary's influence and growing power in the White House were noted by the press. "Significantly she has a larger number of senior officials assigned to her than the vice president, and her personal staff is much more powerful than any previous First Lady's," wrote Margaret Carlson in *Vanity Fair* magazine. "She has five commissioned officers—that is, assistants to the president—in contrast to one for Mrs. Bush."[60]

A personal crisis for the Clintons intervened shortly after Bill took office. In March 1993, Hugh Rodham suffered a stroke in Little Rock. Hillary flew to his side, bringing Chelsea with her, and the two of them sat in the hospital by Hugh's bedside for sixteen straight days, sleeping on cots at night in a spare room that the hospital provided. He died on April 7.

The loss of her father shook Hillary deeply, and she began to privately ponder issues of life and death, and society's role in ensuring the health of its citizens. Health care was on the minds of many Americans, and Hillary was about to take on a political battle on the subject that was unprecedented for a first lady. This effort would color the perception of her in the eyes of many Americans for years to come.

HILLARY TRIES TO REFORM THE NATION'S HEALTH CARE

Bill Clinton had said during the campaign that he wanted to improve health care access and costs for all Americans. He felt that too many Americans could not afford expensive health insurance or treatments and were falling out of the health care system. Shortly after taking office he formed the Health Care Task Force, a commission that would plan and propose sweeping changes to the way all Americans would receive and be charged for health care. He asked Hillary to head the commission and be in charge of health care reform.

It was an unprecedented move. A first lady had never been given such a huge public responsibility. Hillary was suddenly in charge of reforming an area of American life that not only touched people's lives very deeply and personally but accounted for a large part of the nation's economy.

Many Americans, as well as members of the press, disagreed with the appointment of the first lady. They were suspicious of Hillary's influence inside the White House. As Hillary went out into the country to gather information and begin

THE "LAWSUIT-MONGERING FEMINIST"

As Time *magazine reported shortly after the presidential election of 1992, the Republican Party's attacks on Hillary during the campaign were frequent and vicious:*

"The foundations of the anti-Hillary campaign were carefully poured and were part of a larger effort to solidify Bush's conservative base," wrote *Time* reporters. "Republicans dug up—and seriously distorted—some of her old academic articles on children's rights. [One prominent Republican leader] caricatured Hillary as a lawsuit-mongering feminist who likened marriage to slavery and encouraged children to sue their parents. (She did no such thing.) Richard Nixon warned that her forceful intelligence was likely to make her husband 'look like a wimp.' Patrick Buchanan blasted 'Clinton & Clinton' for what he claimed was their agenda of abortion on demand, homosexual rights and putting women in combat."

the difficult process of convincing people and lawmakers to change a system as vast as health care, the personal attacks on her returned. People held up signs demanding to know, "Hillary, Who Elected You President?" Students at colleges passed out bumper stickers that read, "Impeach Hillary." A magazine article mockingly called her "Saint Hillary"; another said that she was the "Czar of Health Care," meaning that she ruled the issue with an iron fist, in the same way that a cruel dictator might rule a country.

Hillary spent most of the next nine months gathering information, running her own staff, and leading the health reform committee. She held private meetings and refused to divulge information to the press, which immediately made them suspicious. Hillary wanted to keep her

findings secret until she could develop a comprehensive health plan, but the press in Washington objected. "Hillary has burrowed deep underground," wrote one reporter. "Her health-care task force began operations in such secrecy that she was sued in federal court and ordered to open the fact-finding meetings."[61]

In October of 1993 Hillary concluded her work on health care reform by delivering a 1,342-page plan to Congress that suggested sweeping changes in the system. She wanted the government to guarantee basic health insurance for all Americans, businesses to pay for health care for their employees, and doctors and specialists to charge far less for their services. Both she and the president made speeches before Congress in support of her plan. It represented dozens of conversations that she had had with doctors, hospital staff, nurses, and people with illnesses, and hundreds of thousands of miles of travel away from her home and family. She had endured criticisms of herself as a wife, mother, and politician that no first lady in history had ever had to face.

What Hillary had failed to do, however, was smooth the way politically for her plan. She had failed to try to muster support for her health care plan by talking with the lawmakers in the House and Senate, enlisting their aid and support and getting them behind the idea. "The scheme was fatally overcomplicated," wrote veteran Washington correspondent James Fallows in the *Atlantic Monthly*. "The proposed legislation, 1,342 pages long, was hard for congress-men to read and impossible for anyone except the plan's creators, Hillary Rodham Clinton and Ira C. Magaziner, to understand."[62]

Hillary's plan was sent into committees for discussion and debate and was quietly and effectively dismissed by Congress. Lawmakers had grown wary of Hillary and recognized that the American public was mistrustful of her efforts to reform health care. A year later, after languishing in committees and never being seriously considered, her plan was officially dismissed without a vote. There would be no major overhaul of the health care system in America during the Clinton administration.

It was a painful lesson in Washington politics for Hillary. Disappointed that the

Hillary Rodham Clinton addresses Congress about health care reform. Congress dismissed the first lady's health care reform bill.

How Hillary Dealt with Personal Attacks

Hillary was generally astonished by the viciousness of the attacks that were leveled at her. When asked by a reporter why she felt that she was such a target for criticism, she jokingly said, "I apparently remind some people of their mother-in-law or their boss, or something." In The Unique Voice of Hillary Rodham Clinton *she goes on to explain how she felt the level of criticism was harmful for the country:*

"I don't mind criticism, and I don't mind controversy, as long as people are criticizing what is being done or said instead of personally attacking each other. I think that's an unfortunate by-product of our politics today where, instead of engaging each other on the merits of an issue and searching for common ground, people stand back and hurl insults at each other. So let's be willing to work together instead of staking out ideological positions and engaging in personal attacks. . . . That's what a democracy thrives on."

task force was unable to make more progress, she has said that the experience brought her to the "school of smaller steps," adding that "we must continue to make progress. It's still important that we increase access to quality health care for working families."[63]

Hillary Looks to Eleanor Roosevelt for Inspiration

Hillary did some soul-searching to try to find a new place for herself and define her role as first lady in a way that would satisfy her own demanding criteria. A psychic counselor whom she invited to the White House suggested that Hillary try to connect with the spirit of Eleanor Roosevelt, the wife of President Franklin D. Roosevelt, who had been a major influence in the White House during the 1940s. Hillary imagined herself talking with Eleanor Roosevelt and found some comfort and direction in considering the former first lady's life of service. Eleanor Roosevelt had also been criticized by the public and the press for being outspoken and for refusing to retreat to a life of hosting White House tea parties. She had traveled extensively around the country and the world and became her husband's "eyes and ears" in the world outside of Washington, D.C.

Hillary returned to the issues of health and women's and children's rights that had always interested her. She read to children who were hospitalized in Washington, D.C., and she began to write a newspaper column about what it was like to be first lady, just as Eleanor Roosevelt had done many years earlier. She became interested in Gulf War Syndrome, a complex series of illnesses that had afflicted servicemen who had fought in the 1991 war against Iraq. After interviewing doctors and servicemen, she presented Bill with a report that became the basis for a task force to study and try to help the servicemen. Hillary was on hand for the announcement of the new task force but, significantly, she was not placed on the committee or asked to oversee it.

The Clintons were the youngest president and first lady that the White House had seen in thirty years, and they loved to have parties and entertain guests. Bill enjoyed having big movie parties, where dozens of people would watch new movies in the White House's theater, including invited guests like actors Warren Beatty and Tom Hanks. The Clintons' youthful style and energy also allowed White House staffers to loosen up. Business suits at meetings were replaced by more casual clothes, such as T-shirts and jeans for men and miniskirts, pants, and bare midriff outfits on some of the

Hillary meets with a group of children from Children's National Medical Center in Washington, D.C. As first lady, she worked to promote women's and children's rights.

women. "As the Clintonites saw it, their arrival marked the victory of youth, enthusiasm and high IQs over the old fogies,"[64] wrote author Joyce Milton.

RAISING CHELSEA IN THE WHITE HOUSE

Hillary made sure that she always had time to spend with Chelsea, who became a teenager in the White House. Bill and Hillary were devoted parents who tried to raise Chelsea as "normally" as could be expected under the intense scrutiny of the White House. Hillary was there to do homework with her daughter, and she and Bill tried to have dinner at home most evenings. "There is no better time to catch up on what we have been doing all day, what we are excited about, and what troubles us," Hillary wrote. "This evening, for instance, Bill talked about the budget debate in Congress and Chelsea talked about her history paper. Together, we talked about plans for Thanksgiving."[65]

Chelsea went to a private school and, as is customary for children of the president, had secret service escorts wherever she went. But she also enjoyed some benefits from her parents' unique position that not many kids ever experience. During the course of Bill's presidency, Chelsea had seventy-two sleepover guests at the White House, all carefully registered and noted in the official logbooks that the government is required to keep.

Hillary also made sure that Chelsea was excluded from the intense media coverage in the nation's capital. From an early age Chelsea had been taught by her parents that criticism and outright accusations were a part of the life of a politician and that she should not believe everything that was published in the newspapers about her famous parents. "When I was growing up, my parents always told me that I had to do what I thought was right and not listen to other people," Hillary told a reporter. "That was hard for me. And I didn't have one-millionth of the attention that she'll have. But both of us are going to try to tell her the same thing that our parents told us and to try to help her understand how she can become the person she is meant to be."[66]

Chelsea was also able to travel with her mother. In 1994, when Chelsea was fourteen, she and Hillary embarked on an exotic trip to the Far East, where they visited India, Pakistan, and Bangladesh, among other countries, rode elephants, visited Muslim mosques, and toured the famous Taj Mahal palace.

HILLARY WRITES *IT TAKES A VILLAGE*

In 1995 Hillary was approached by a publisher to write a book that would sum up her experiences and research on the issue of children's health and well-being. She had been accumulating data and information about women's and children's issues ever since her college days at Wellesley and Yale and during all of the years that she was involved with the Children's Defense Fund. Working with a Washing-

Chelsea and Hillary pose in front of the Taj Mahal in India. Chelsea and her mother traveled extensively, visiting places like India, Pakistan, and Bangladesh.

ton, D.C., ghostwriter, Hillary plunged into the task of organizing and writing *It Takes a Village: And Other Lessons Children Teach Us*. After many revisions and corrections the book was published the following year and became an instant success.

The main point of Hillary's book was that children are influenced by a variety of factors as they grow up, and the "village" of caregivers—whether they are ministers, teachers, parents, grandpar-

ents, or friends and neighbors—is vital in looking after the upbringing of the nation's children.

"Children are not rugged individualists," Hillary wrote. "They depend on the adults they know and on thousands more who make decisions every day that affect their well-being."[67] In a text that was in large part a call to society to change its policies regarding children's health and welfare, she wrote about social programs that had been successful in helping children, and she delivered statistics about issues like day-care and nutrition. That was the easy part for Hillary, who always knew the issues and the research inside out. The tough part was relating her own experience and showing her human side, both in stories about her upbringing in Illinois and about how she and Bill raised Chelsea. Mothers could relate to Hillary's stories about learning how to breast-feed her newborn daughter and how she had had to return to the doctor five days after giving birth because of an infection.

The book was a hit, staying on the best-sellers' list for twenty weeks and earning over $1 million, which Hillary donated to charities dedicated to children and families. She recorded the book for an audio version that was also popular, and later that year she won a Grammy Award for the best spoken-word recording of the year. She and the president attended a star-studded awards ceremony at Madison Square Garden in New York. Hillary was dressed in a beautiful gown by Oscar de la Renta and looked every part the star of the show.

Later during her tenure as first lady, she collected the letters that kids sent to the White House into a book entitled *Dear Socks, Dear Buddy: Kids' Letters to the First Pets*. Proceeds from that book were given to the National Park Foundation. Her final book as first lady was titled *An Invitation to the White House: At Home with History*. It recounts the history of the great mansion and its role in welcoming the people of the world. Hillary dedicated the

---

BILL AS A GAS STATION ATTENDANT?

A joke that made the rounds on the Internet after the presidential election, recounted here by author Gail Sheehy, demonstrates the influence that people felt Hillary had on Bill:

"President Clinton and the First Lady are out driving in the country near Hillary's hometown. Bill asks that the presidential limousine pull into the nearest gas station. The attendant catches a glimpse of the First Lady. 'Hey, Hillary, remember me?' he says. 'We used to date in high school.' They chat for a few minutes.

As the First Couple is driven away, Bill is feeling very proud of himself. He looks over at Hillary. 'You used to date that guy? Just think what it would be like if you had married *him*,' he says smugly.

Hillary shrugs. 'If I'd married him, *you'd* be pumping gas, and *he'd* be President.'"

Hillary displays a copy of An Invitation to the White House, *one of several books she wrote while her husband was in office.*

book "to the American people, whose commitment to democracy has made this house more than a home; and to the White House staff, whose dedication has made a home of this venerable house."[68]

Besides providing an inside look at the inner workings of the White House, the book may also serve as a scrapbook for Hillary and some of her happier moments in Washington. There are photos of her and Bill appearing in costumes at parties, Bill dancing with a young Chelsea, and the family opening Christmas presents.

HILLARY BECOMES A VOICE FOR WOMEN'S ISSUES AROUND THE WORLD

It was also in 1995 that Hillary took on another role that would vault her to international prominence and become her most endearing legacy in the White House. She was invited to speak at the United Nations Fourth World Conference on Women, which was held in Beijing, China. It was a major event that brought together influential women from all around the world to discuss ways of granting more individual rights and freedoms to women, and Hillary was determined to make a strong statement.

Wearing a pink suit, Hillary strode to the microphone in a massive hall and began to speak. She declared that although women made up more than half of the world's population, they were denied basic rights in many countries. Even in developed countries, women's rights and choices were not respected, she added. She condemned governments that denied basic rights, such as her Chinese hosts, who cracked down on free speech, and she launched into a bitter attack on the abuses of women that are accepted as normal in some countries around the world.

Her speech was met with thunderous applause by the thousands of women delegates in attendance. It would have a resounding impact around the world, as women returned to their countries and, emboldened by Hillary's words, began to demand changes in their own societies. "Beijing unleashed something extraordinary: pressure by activists all around the world on behalf of women,"[69] said one Clinton staffer. It also unleashed something extraordinary in Hillary: She had begun to see how to use her position as first lady to make the kinds of positive changes in the world, of which she had always dreamt.

By the end of Bill Clinton's administration, Hillary had traveled overseas sixty-two times, exceeding the number of countries visited by her globe-trotting idol, Eleanor Roosevelt, during her lifetime. Hillary had become an ambassador to the entire world, tirelessly advocating women's rights and demonstrating by her presence and charisma the opportunities that a modern, liberated woman could seize.

By the time that Bill Clinton was reelected for a second term in office, Hillary's popularity had returned. She was a sought-after speaker and a tireless campaigner on behalf of Democratic candidates across the country. She had managed to weather many storms in Washington, but the biggest scandal of the Clinton administration was about to break. And with it would come one of the major crises of Hillary's life, as she battled to regain control of her life and her marriage.

5 Scandal and Denial

I sometimes don't know what I've been accused of from day to day.

—*Hillary, on turmoil in the White House*

In many ways the Clintons were prepared for the kinds of personal attacks and criticism that they would face in Washington, D.C. Because of her work, her surname, and her public advocacy, Hillary had faced criticism during the years that Bill was governor of Arkansas. In 1986, when Bill was running for reelection as governor, an opponent had promised that his own wife would be a "full-time First Lady" and questioned Hillary's work in relationship to the state government. At that time, Bill was able to diffuse the accusations by saying in a speech, "Remember, Frank, you're running for governor, not First Lady."[70] He took a similar stance during the presidential campaign, when he reminded the Republicans, and George Bush in particular, that they were running against Bill, not Hillary.

If the Clintons thought that their critics would be silenced after his resounding victory in the 1992 election, they were sorely mistaken. In fact things would get far worse. Bill Clinton's first years in office were punctuated by running scandals and accusations, many of them directed squarely at the first lady. Questions were raised about the couple's finances, Hillary's business practices over the years at the Rose Law Firm, the business ethics of her former friends and associates in Arkansas, and the decisions that she made during her first months in the White House.

Some of the questions were raised by Republicans who were furious that Clinton had won the presidency and suspicious of Hillary's influence on the shaping of the government. At other times the press dug for information that cast a critical light on the Clintons, and when they found out that Hillary in particular was unwilling to divulge information, they grew even more suspicious of her and tried harder to find damaging information. In the end most of the allegations were dismissed as being without merit and the Clintons were never charged with any crimes—but only after millions of public dollars were spent on investigations and hundreds of articles appeared in the nation's media detailing the charges against the Clintons.

There was one scandal that did stick, however. Bill Clinton had been accused for many years of having illicit sexual affairs and relationships outside of his marriage. When questioned, he denied the affairs or claimed that the women in question were exaggerating their relationships with him. Toward the end of his presidency, however, one affair with a young White House intern named Monica Lewinsky could not be covered up. The resulting firestorm of lurid details, denial, and finally the truth would be the biggest scandal of all and would lead to Bill Clinton's impeachment.

Hillary had to weather these storms, too, and her defense of her husband through every kind of accusation had a profound effect on how the nation viewed her. She gave explanations and defenses of her own conduct that were unprecedented in the history of first ladies in Washington. During the Clinton presidency, Hillary was called upon to defend

Bill Clinton's involvement with White House intern Monica Lewinsky led to his impeachment. Lewinsky appears with her attorney shortly after her relationship with Clinton was revealed.

"Do You Let the Bad Times Outweigh the Good?"

Even when she was faced with controversy and accusations as first lady, Hillary always felt that she had to put her life, and the criticisms, in their proper perspective. In this excerpt from a Vanity Fair *magazine article from 1994, she told writer Leslie Bennetts how she overcomes adversity:*

"I like my life," [Hillary] says defiantly. "I am just grateful for all the opportunities I've had, and along with the good comes a lot of hard parts. . . . I think there are points in each person's life when you face a turning point. Do you become overwhelmed by whatever life has dealt you? Do you let the bad times outweigh all the good? Do you give in to anger or bitterness or insecurity, or do you fight against that? I mean, we all have that choice every day. Each one of us has those challenges."

herself, her past, her marriage, and her very identity as a mother and wife.

HILLARY IS ACCUSED OF "TRAVELGATE"

The White House has a department that coordinates all of the travel schedules of the president, the first lady, and the dozens of reporters and aides who accompany the president on official trips. The staff of the department makes sure that there are enough seats on chartered airplanes and buses to accommodate everyone who has legitimate business following the White House entourage, and a significant amount of money is spent to make the operation run smoothly.

Early in 1993, just a few months after Bill took office, a friend of the Clinton's named Harry Thomason was asked to investigate the management of the Travel Office. Complaints had been made that the office was not being managed properly, and Thomason, after closer review, reported that the office appeared to have financial discrepancies and errors in accounting. As Hillary later said, "There was petty cash left lying around. Cash ended up in the personal account of one of the workers. . . . Even if it was just the press's money, that money belongs to people and it should be handled appropriately if it is in any way connected with the White House."[71] Seven staff members from the department—at least one of whom had worked there over thirty years—were fired from their jobs.

But it did not stop there. The seven fired employees were subsequently investigated by the FBI to see if they had committed any criminal acts while employed by the government, such as stealing money or using their positions to get favors for their friends or relatives. This infuriated the Republican opposition in Washington, who felt that not only had the seven employees, who had worked in the Travel Office under President Bush, been fired unjustly, but that the new White House was using the FBI illegally to try to drum up false charges against the employees. In July Republican senator Bob Dole asked for a special investigation into what was being called "Travelgate"—a veiled reference to the Watergate scandal that had brought down President Richard Nixon years earlier.

Hillary was accused of having some part in the firings and the resultant heavy-handed investigation of the employees. Such a role was not part of the first lady's official duties, and the press was quick to suggest that she had overstepped her office. She denied that she had ordered the firings or the investigation, but speculation was rampant that Hillary had used her influence in the White House to wield power. "Although I had no decision-making role with regard to the removal of the Travel Office employees," she said in a carefully worded statement, "I expressed my concern . . . that if there were fiscal mismanagement in the Travel Office or in any part of the White House it should be addressed promptly."[72]

The firings had been officially carried out by Vincent Foster, a former colleague of Hillary's at the Rose Law Firm in Arkansas and a close friend of the Clintons for many years. Hillary refused to answer questions from reporters about the matter, which made them more suspicious that she was hiding something. The pressure on Foster to tell the whole truth about the firings and about who had ordered the FBI investigation built up. At the same time, investigators and the media were beginning to question Foster about Whitewater, a former land deal in Arkansas that the Rose Law Firm, including Hillary, had been involved with years earlier.

The pressure on Foster became unbearable. On July 20, Vincent Foster, one of Hillary's closest friends and business partners, committed suicide at a public park in Washington, D.C. Shortly after his death many files related to the Travel Office and the Whitewater investigation were removed from his office.

SUSPICIONS OF HILLARY'S INFLUENCE DEEPEN

The Travelgate scandal never did reveal any crimes, but it raised questions in the press and the public about Hillary's influence in the White House. The feeling among Washington insiders, particularly opponents of the Clintons, was not that Bill and Hillary had done nothing wrong. People believed very strongly that the Clintons were simply very good at hiding their mistakes and covering up illegal acts. As one *Newsweek* reporter put it, "[Hillary's] distrust of the press has become obsessive and politically risky. Her stonewalling has lent further credence to the speculation that the Clintons have something to hide."[73]

An image had been cast of Hillary as someone who would stop at nothing to get what she wanted in the behind-the-scenes struggle for power inside the White House, and that image would not be easily dispelled. Stories about Travelgate were thick and heavy in the press for several months, along with speculation about what led to Vincent Foster's suicide. Across the country, even more "Impeach Hillary" signs were being displayed. The first lady had started off her reign in Washington badly, and the people of America would be slow to forgive her.

The press began to write stories that tried to explain Hillary's behavior and personality. At times the stories were both critical and admiring of her. "Mrs. Clinton's pride is matched by her immense discipline, a strength that allows her to put aside her troubles as if by sheer effort of will,"[74] wrote Leslie Bennetts in *Vanity Fair*. As Hillary's friend television producer Linda Bloodworth-Thomason said, "She's got this monumental tolerance for adversity, and that makes people mad, too. People want to see her cry, and they won't get to. That doesn't mean she won't cry, but she's very private, and she won't cry for any of her detractors."[75]

THE WHITEWATER PROBE

As the Clinton administration's first year in office came to a close, the White House was rocked by a new scandal that would take years to investigate and dominate

Senator Bob Dole and the first lady meet at the White House. In 1993 Dole called for an investigation into Hillary's role in the Travelgate scandal.

HILLARY MAKES PEACE WITH THE PRESS

Hillary's press conference of April 1994 was one of her first attempts to work with the press rather than to deny them information. In the case of Time *magazine, the strategy seemed to work, as she received this glowing review of her appearance:*

"Most reporters had been waiting 3½ months to fire questions at the First Lady about Whitewater. What happened was a riveting hour and 12 minutes in which the First Lady appeared to be open, candid, but above all unflappable. While she provided little new information on the tangled Arkansas land deal or her controversial commodity trades, the real message was her attitude and her poise. The confiding tone and relaxed body language, which was seen live on four networks, immediately drew approving reviews."

the headlines for the remainder of Bill Clinton's presidency. Questions were being raised, initially by reporters for the *New York Times* and *Washington Post* newspapers, about an old land deal in Arkansas that had failed and lost a lot of money for a lot of people. The deal had been called Whitewater, for a proposed new community alongside the White River that had never been built. Bill and Hillary had been investors in the deal in 1978, at the time that Bill had run for and won his first term as Arkansas's governor. Hillary's law firm had worked with the developers of Whitewater, who were also involved in a failed savings and loan business that had lost millions of investors' dollars. Jim McDougal, a close friend and former business associate of the Clintons had gone to jail for stealing money in similar land-development schemes.

The press demanded to know how deeply the Clintons had been involved in the Whitewater fiasco and if they had benefited financially from the failed deal. They pointed out that the scandal, and what they believed to be a White House cover-up, pointed as much to Hillary as it did to Bill. "Four of the 10 officials subpoenaed to testify on their efforts to manage the Whitewater scandal are Hillary's employees or allies,"[76] wrote a *Newsweek* reporter. The press wanted access to all of the Clintons' records about the deal, stretching back fifteen years, and they wanted the Clintons to ask the Rose Law Firm to open their own records on the savings and loan case, as well as other cases with which Hillary had been involved, for public inspection. Clinton opponents were convinced that it would be revealed that the Clintons had used their influence in Arkansas to help defraud investors of millions of dollars.

At first Bill and Hillary said that they barely remembered Whitewater and had nothing to hide. "It's a little bit odd that in my twenty years of law practice and involvement in so many activities, you know, I'm getting grilled over what I did, which amounted to about an hour of work over each week over fifteen months, and it was by no means important or significant to me at the time,"[77] Hillary complained.

As the clamor continued, Bill called for an independent commission to oversee the investigation of Whitewater. In January 1994 Attorney General Janet Reno named Democrat Robert Fiske to head the investigation. The press learned that an important set of files related to Whitewater had mysteriously disappeared from the Rose Law Firm offices, and suspicions of the Clintons' influence in the case deepened.

In April of that year Hillary called a rare press conference to dispel rumors that she and the administration were trying to obstruct the investigation. She answered questions about Whitewater and the allegations of a White House cover-up. She said that much of the confusion about Whitewater was "really a result of our inexperience in Washington."[78] She promised to try to be more understanding of the press and its persistent pushing for answers. When a *Newsweek* reporter asked Hillary if she was angry about allegations that she and Bill were corrupt, she said, "I'm very sad about it. But I also have a full life to live. I'm still my husband's wife, I'm still Chelsea's mother. I'm still involved in a lot of other activities that are important to me and my family. So I don't really get the luxury of expending too much energy being angry with people who are being unfair and untruthful."[79]

The president's opponents wanted a totally independent commission established to investigate Whitewater, and they lobbied Congress hard to create one. In August 1994 Congress authorized an independent investigation of Whitewater and named Republican Kenneth Starr to lead it. The investigation would last for five more years, cost nearly $50 million in public money to conduct, and involve more than four hundred people, one hundred of whom were White House officials. The Clintons themselves, as well as many of their friends who were implicated in the scandal, would incur more than $23 million in legal bills to defend themselves. Hillary herself would be called upon to testify before a grand jury, the first time in history that a first lady was forced to testify in a legal forum. In the end there were no arrests or criminal sanctions handed down from the Whitewater investigation.

A statement that Hillary made in March 1994 to a *Newsweek* reporter seemed prophetic. "People are going to spend millions and millions of dollars and they're going to conclude we made a bad land investment,"[80] she said.

QUESTIONS ABOUT THE PRESIDENT'S INFIDELITIES

The critics and enemies of the Clinton administration felt that with Whitewater they had begun to establish a pattern of lying and deceit by the president and first lady. Their next attack was on the president's personal life and conduct in private. It was also in 1994 that a woman named Paula Corbin Jones came forward to tell her story to the American public. A former state clerk from Arkansas, Jones said that Bill Clinton had made unwelcome sexual advances to her years earlier when Clinton was still the governor of Arkansas. She wanted an apology from the president. Bill denied that he had ever done anything wrong and claimed that he did not even know who she was. Jones filed a lawsuit against the president, but most people felt that it was politically motivated and intended solely as a way to discredit the president. At the time the matter became little more than fodder for gossip columns and speculation in the press.

Questions about the president's infidelities were nothing new. One such scandal had nearly stopped the first Clinton presidential campaign in its tracks. Early in the running, a young woman named Gennifer Flowers was paid a large sum of money by a tabloid newspaper to reveal that she had had a romantic relationship for twelve years with the governor of Arkansas. The Clinton staff knew that the American public would not support a candidate who appeared to be immoral, and the campaign headquarters went into serious damage control over the Flowers revelation. Candidate Clinton denied the affair, and he and Hillary went on the national television news show *60 Minutes* to dispute the allegations.

HILLARY'S WHITEWATER NURSERY RHYME

During the Whitewater investigation, Hillary was fond of quoting this nursery rhyme: "As I was standing in the street as quiet as could be / A great big ugly man came up and tied his horse to me." As author Gail Sheehy points out in Hillary's Choice, *the simple rhyme had a very direct meaning for the first lady:*

"The man was, of course, Kenneth Starr. The 'I' was the way Hillary saw herself: working behind the scenes on issues and principles and selflessly helping her husband to regain the reins of a presidency run amok. Why, then, was this zealot chasing her down and trying to tie his subpoena to her? It was an infuriating distraction from her efforts to use the power of her husband's office to change things for the better for Americans and for women and children around the world."

Paula Jones talks with reporters about her sexual harassment lawsuit against President Bill Clinton.

The Paula Jones case was not as easily dismissed. She continued to press her cause. By 1997 she had fired her lawyers and obtained new legal representation to pursue her claim that Bill Clinton had sexually harassed her. She had also received the financial backing of a conservative group that wanted to discredit the president. The Jones case was taken up by Kenneth Starr, the special prosecutor who had expanded his Whitewater investigation to include other issues related to the Clintons. He declared that the Jones case established a pattern of lying and deception by the president that had to be investigated on behalf of the American people.

Starr began to investigate all of the rumors about Bill's infidelities that had swirled in Washington over the years. One woman after another, most with roots in Arkansas, was called to the nation's capital to testify about romantic links to the president during his long political career. Some of the women reluctantly admitted their relationships, and many flat-out denied ever having had sexual relations with Bill. The White House and Clinton's spokespeople dismissed all of the charges.

THE MONICA LEWINSKY AFFAIR

One woman was called to testify who was not a ghost from Bill Clinton's distant past. Her name was Monica Lewinsky, and she had only recently ended an affair with the president. Or rather, the president had ended it with her. Lewinsky was a twenty-two-year-old White House intern, barely older than Chelsea Clinton, when she began to have intimate "dates" with the president in the Oval Office of the White House. The affair lasted several months during Bill's successful campaign for reelection in 1996, and Lewinsky was given a job in the White House. The president called her frequently and bestowed several small gifts upon her, including a copy of Walt Whitman's *Leaves of Grass*, a book that he had once given Hillary when they were dating.

Lewinsky was upset when the president wanted the affair to end. Staffers who were trying to protect the president even had Lewinsky transferred from her White House job to another one at the Pentagon in order to get her as far away from the president as possible. Lewinsky began to complain about Bill to her friend Linda Tripp, who also worked in the White House. Tripp suggested that Lewinsky begin to secretly tape-record her conversations with the president and to keep some of the evidence of their relationship. The records showed that Lewinsky visited the White House three dozen times even after her transfer to the Pentagon, and even though she claimed they were for official business or visits to her old friends, the evidence of an illicit affair was leading straight back to the president.

Armed with tapes of intimate conversations between the president and Lewinsky, Linda Tripp brought the evidence to Kenneth Starr's attention. The prosecutor finally had irrefutable evidence of the president's infidelity, and he set a legal trap for President Clinton. On January 17, 1998, a little over a year after the president had begun his second term in office, he was called in to make a legal deposition, or statement, to Starr's grand jury. He was asked questions about the alleged affairs with women, and he denied that he had had affairs or that he had ever tried to cover up his illicit relationships or that he had paid women to stay silent. When Lewinsky's name was raised, he specifically denied ever having had sexual relations with her.

But this time there was proof that the president was lying. Although it was not illegal to have illicit romantic affairs, it was illegal to lie to a grand jury, and Starr had finally caught the president in a lie.

On the morning of January 21, when the story broke in the *Washington Post* newspaper, Hillary was awakened by Bill, who said, "You're not going to believe this, but—I want to tell you what's in the newspapers."[81] He warned her that the story would accuse him of having an affair and of lying about it to the grand jury. Hillary would later say that he did not admit that day to having the affair and that she did not press him for details or the truth.

Hillary tried to defend her husband. She said that the charges against Bill were all false and tried to portray Lewinsky as a wide-eyed kid who had only thought the president was lavishing special attention on her. On an appearance on the *Today Show*, the first lady said that the gifts to

Lewinsky were simply the act of a generous man. "Anyone who knows my husband knows that he is an extremely generous person to people he knows, to strangers, to anybody who is around him," she said. "And I think that . . . his treatment of people will certainly explain all of this." She went on to complain that there was a "vast, right-wing conspiracy"[82] that had been trying for years to bring down the president, and the Lewinsky affair was just a part of it.

BILL IS IMPEACHED FOR LYING

The evidence of the sexual affair between the president and Lewinsky was too clear to dismiss. Kenneth Starr sent a report to Congress that the president had lied and tried to obstruct the investigation of the Lewinsky affair, and offered eleven different points as grounds for impeachment. The Republican-dominated House of Representatives debated the issue throughout most of the year, and on December 19,

Kenneth Starr recommends to Congress that President Clinton be impeached. In December 1998 the House of Representatives voted to impeach the president.

1998, nearly a year after the scandal had broken, representatives voted for two articles of impeachment to remove Bill Clinton from office. One article charged that the president had perjured himself (or lied) when he denied having the affair to Starr's grand jury; the other article charged him with obstructing justice during the investigation of the affair.

The attacks on the president and first lady were partisan and vicious. Hillary would later acknowledge that when Bill finally told her the truth about the affair in August of that year, it was the most difficult time of her life. In *Living History*, a book that she wrote in 2003 about her years as first lady, she wrote, "I could hardly breathe. Gulping for air, I started crying and and yelling at him, 'What do you mean? . . . Why did you lie to me?' I was furious and getting more so by the second. He just stood there saying over and over again, 'I'm sorry. I'm so sorry. I was trying to protect you and Chelsea.'"[83]

The final vote to remove the president rested with the Democrat-controlled Senate. For two agonizing months they debated the issue. In February 1999 the Senate finally held its vote: Conviction on both charges was denied and the scandal-ridden Clinton presidency was spared.

HILLARY IS VIEWED IN A NEW LIGHT

Many people wondered openly if Hillary would, or should, divorce her husband and leave Washington and the White House. Others wondered if she had known all along about Monica Lewinsky and all of the other women who had shared Bill Clinton's life and if she had conspired to cover up the affairs, too. Authors and newspaper columnists tried to psychoanalyze Hillary in print and figure out how she could maintain her support for Bill and her marriage. They wondered if Hillary simply pretended that everything in her world was okay in order to protect herself.

Hillary did not discuss the incident publicly for many years. It was not until the summer of 2003 that she revealed the strain that the Lewinsky affair had had on her marriage. She recalled in her book, *Living History*, that during a summer vacation in 1998 with Bill and Chelsea, she had felt "nothing but profound sadness, disappointment and unresolved anger. I could not talk to Bill, and when I did, it was a tirade."[84]

The experience had certainly changed the first lady. In the eyes of the public, Bill's betrayal of her and her decision to stay by his side had somehow softened Hillary and made her more likeable. Perhaps she seemed more like a real person who faced the harsher aspects of life with some dignity and inner courage, and they admired that.

Like her husband, who survived the first impeachment proceedings in Washington in 130 years, Hillary weathered the storm of controversy. Speculation had already begun that she would seek political office in 2000 when the Clinton presidency ended. Her name began to come up as a possible candidate, and as the election season began in 1999, there were many people who wanted Hillary to achieve yet another first for a first lady: She could be the first one ever to attempt to run for office on her own merits.

As Gail Sheehy wrote in *Hillary's Choice*, "The most ironic turn of the Clintons' twisted relationship was still ahead: As the world's most publicly degraded wife, Hillary, by choosing to stay with her husband, would levitate far above him."[85]

6 Senator Clinton

You have to try to stand for something bigger than yourself.

—Hillary

By the summer of 1998 Hillary had become the top attraction in the Democratic Party and a sought-after speaker and fund-raiser. She campaigned hard that year on behalf of Democratic candidates across the country who were running for seats in the U.S. Congress. Campaigning in twenty states, she attended fifty fund-raisers and spoke at thirty-four rallies, a dizzying pace for any candidate, much less a first lady. Her efforts were credited for securing wins for Democratic candidates in close races in New York State and California.

Jesse Jackson, a family friend of the Clintons and a spiritual adviser to them when the Monica Lewinsky scandal erupted, had nothing but praise for Hillary. At a campaign rally in Chicago, he said, "Hillary, you've come through rain and you're not wet. You've walked through fire and there's not a singe on your clothing."[86]

In other words Hillary had come through the scandals of her husband's administration unscathed. Her dignity was intact, and her loyalty to her marriage and to the political process was admired by the American public. The polls indicated that her popularity was at an all-time high, which was noticed by the leadership of the Democratic Party in Washington. They began to view her as a potential candidate, and this time the first lady, who had always shunned the idea of running for office, was willing to listen.

HILLARY DECLARES HER CANDIDACY FOR THE SENATE

Three days after the elections of 1998 were completed, Senator Daniel Patrick Moynihan of New York State made a surprise announcement. He would not run for reelection in the year 2000 and would instead relinquish the seat in the U.S. Senate that he had held for twenty-four years. Politicians in New York immediately began to explore the possibility of running for Moynihan's prestigious position.

Hillary had appeared several times in New York on behalf of Charles Schumer, the Democrat who had unseated Republican senator Al D'Amato for the other Senate seat from New York State. Schumer and others saw that Hillary wielded tremendous influence in the state, despite never having lived there. As author Michael Tomasky wrote, "If there was any Democrat to whom [Schumer] owed a debt, any Democrat who had rallied voters to his cause . . . it was the woman New York voters seemed to listen to above anyone else. It was Hillary Rodham Clinton."[87]

Hillary was not a prototypical senatorial candidate. Although she had been active in all of Bill's political campaigns

Daniel Patrick Moynihan and Hillary walk together at the senator's home in New York. Hillary won Moynihan's seat in the Senate after his retirement.

and had spoken publicly on many political issues, she had never actually run for political office. Most Senate candidates had established voting records. Hillary did not. She also had little personal wealth to use in a campaign. In fact the Clintons had to solicit donations from wealthy Democrats to pay the legal bills that they had incurred defending themselves against the Whitewater charges. Finally, no first lady in history had ever run for office, least of all when her husband was still in office.

Hillary did not even live in the state of New York. She had always enjoyed the bustling atmosphere of New York City and hoped to move there after her years in the White House were completed, but she could not claim any special allegiance to the state. In the summer of 1999 the Clintons solved that problem by buying a nineteenth-century home in the quiet town of Chappaqua, New York, a forty-minute drive from Manhattan. It had a pool and a spacious yard, and it reminded Hillary in many ways of her childhood home in Park Ridge, Illinois.

A month later, on July 8, 1999, Hillary announced that she would begin a campaign for the U.S. Senate. The announcement came at the pastoral farmhouse of Senator Moynihan in a rural part of west-central New York State. The retiring senator introduced and endorsed Hillary for his seat. "I may be new to the neighborhood," she said of her recent move to the state, "but I'm not new to the concerns of New Yorkers."[88]

Hillary immediately set out on a summer-long tour of the state, where she met with local politicians and dignitaries in small groups, introducing herself to them and beginning to study the issues that would define her campaign. Of what came to be known as her "listening and learning tour," she said, "I think I have some real work to do to get out and listen and learn from the people of New York and demonstrate that what I'm for is maybe as important—if not more important—than where I'm from."[89]

BUMPS ALONG THE CAMPAIGN TRAIL

The campaign did not start out smoothly for Hillary. Critics were quick to call her a "carpetbagger," a derisive word for an out-of-towner who arrives in a new place and begins to drain its assets. The press, which had viewed Hillary with suspicion ever since her early days in the White House, questioned whether she was trustworthy. As a writer for the *New Yorker* magazine put it, "How does someone mount a Senate campaign from a state where she has never lived if she has no record of accomplishment to point to and is, on top of all that, widely distrusted?"[90]

At the beginning of her campaign Hillary did nothing to allay the mistrust of the press. She refused to grant one-on-one interviews, and she frequently instructed her staff to keep journalists at a distance from her during appearances. At times she slipped in and out of appearances without allowing photos to

Hillary greets supporters urging her to run for the U.S. Senate.

be taken or questions to be asked, which further eroded her relationship with the working press that was assigned to cover her campaign.

Hillary had good reason to be wary of the media. When given the chance, they pressed her with personal questions about her marriage and the Monica Lewinsky affair. Hillary was very cautious with her answers and resorted to talking only about policy issues. "Literally hundreds of journalists show up whenever she does anything the slightest bit noteworthy, and when she is in control of the agenda she uses the occasion to say at some length almost nothing,"[91] complained one writer.

In the case of voters, people had developed different images of Hillary from what they had read about her in the press for the last eight years. Many saw her as a symbol of what they believed to be wrong about American society, rather than as a person. To succeed in her campaign, Hillary had to make people see her as someone who cared about their lives and their problems. "[Her success] will depend . . . on whether she can defeat people's fiercely held preconceptions and compel them to think of her in a new and more complex way," predicted one scribe. "Most candidates don't have to demonstrate to people that they're human beings. But most candidates aren't Hillary."[92]

Hillary persevered. She saw in New York State a real need for change, especially in the areas of health and education, which were her specialties. She insisted on talking only about the issues, and when she agreed to interviews with the media, she ignored questions about the scandals that had erupted in the White House during the Clinton presidency. "What's important to me are the issues," she said at one press conference. "I mean, who, at the end of the day, is going to improve education for the children of New York? Who's going to improve health care for the people of New York? Who's going to bring people together? And that's what I'm going to be talking about."[93] She canvassed the entire state, traveling to all sixty-two counties to meet with local people, gather in their concerns, and formulate plans for addressing the needs of all New Yorkers.

Assured of the Democratic nomination, Hillary had to wait to see who would oppose her from the Republican Party. The leading Republican candidate appeared to be Rudolph Giuliani, the tough mayor of New York City who had already begun to openly criticize Hillary. Applauded by New Yorkers for cracking down hard on crime, he was known for being blunt and fiercely combative. Observers expected a close and contentious race between the two candidates. In May 2000, however,

HILLARY'S VIEW ON THE NECESSITY OF POLITICS

At a commencement address at Drew University, Hillary offered a rationale for her own unique view of politics, as reported in Claire Osborne's The Unique Voice of Hillary Rodham Clinton:

"I don't mean to suggest that government is perfect by any means. The practice of politics and governing has never been easy. . . . Politics is not just about who's elected to office. Politics is how we get along with one another. How we compromise with each other. When someone says to me, 'How can you stand being involved in politics?', I always say, 'Are you married? Do you have a family? Do you belong to a church or school?' Because politics with a small *p* is that process that brings us together peaceably to work toward common ends."

During a debate, Rick Lazio demands that Hillary Rodham Clinton sign a pledge to limit campaign contributions. This aggressive challenge proved detrimental to Lazio's campaign.

Giuliani announced that he had been diagnosed with a form of cancer. He withdrew himself from the race, eliminating the largest obstacle to Hillary's campaign. In his place the Republicans named Rick Lazio, a U.S. congressman from Long Island, to oppose Hillary in the general election.

HILLARY WINS THE ELECTION IN A LANDSLIDE

Lazio and Hillary campaigned hard throughout the summer and fall of 2000 and debated each other three times. At the end of one debate Lazio rushed over to Hillary's podium and waved a piece of paper in her face that he wanted her to sign on the spot, pledging to limit campaign contributions. Hillary coolly ignored the challenge, and voters sided overwhelmingly with Hillary against the "space invader," as Lazio was called for aggressively confronting her. It was a major blunder on his part that turned the momentum of the campaign in Hillary's favor.

Hillary resisted using her celebrity as a major focus of her campaign. Instead she stuck to the issues, and as the campaign went on, she made more and more of a connection with voters. She became successful at transforming herself in their eyes into a caring person, and not a symbol of embattled women or rigid feminism. "Journalists continued to find her infuriating and opaque," wrote Tomasky toward the end of the campaign.

Voters . . . were arriving at a very different conclusion. The woman who a year before tended to enter and leave rooms through private doors was now charging into crowds and establishing a rapport with her audiences. Everywhere she went, she worked every rope line and shook every hand and posed for every picture.[94]

The people of New York came to believe in the candidate. On election night, November 7, 2000, they voted Hillary into

HILLARY'S SENATE CAMPAIGN TRANSFORMED HER INTO A "PEOPLE PERSON"

Hillary came a long way in her ability to interact closely with the public, as Patrick Halley reports in his book On the Road with Hillary. *In this anecdote Hillary is working a crowd during her Senate campaign in New York:*

"The Hillary I'd worked with as first lady would have waved politely and retreated to her limousine. Hillary the Senate candidate waded into the crowd with gusto, shaking hands and posing for countless snapshots. Then she surveyed the street, suggested we visit some of the other merchants, and proceeded to go from store to store saying hello. When she reached the end of the block, she stopped and let the reporters gather around. . . . Hillary hated being mobbed, and the press was the worst. Now she was inviting it. My, how things had changed."

Hillary's new, friendly demeanor helped her win the 2000 New York Senate race.

As a freshman senator, Hillary was appointed to serve on several important senate committees.

office by a resounding 55 percent margin and more than eight hundred thousand votes over Lazio. One of the votes cast for her was by her daughter, Chelsea, now twenty years old and a registered voter in New York. Another was by Bill, the president of the country. In her victory speech, Hillary said "I promise you tonight that I will reach across party lines to bring progress for all of New York's families." Employing a bit of New York jargon, which endeared her even more to her supporters, she then said, "I just *wanna* say from the bottom of my heart: Thank you New York!"[95]

HILLARY BEGINS HER CAREER AS A SENATOR

In January 2001 Hillary was one of eleven freshman senators who began their six-year terms in Washington, D.C. She bought and furnished a large townhouse in the exclusive Georgetown neighborhood to be her and Bill's second home.

She adapted smoothly to her role as the junior senator from New York State and surprised many people by fitting in easily with her fellow senators, many of whom had criticized her and Bill harshly during his presidency. At first she and her staff occupied a suite of offices in the basement of the Russell Senate Office Building, but she was soon moved upstairs to a handsome suite of offices that she had painted her favorite color, yellow.

In her first year in office, Hillary was appointed to serve on three important Senate committees: Budget, Environment and Public works, and Health, Education, Labor, and Pensions. Both positions allowed Hillary to continue her passionate advocacy on behalf of women and children. Fulfilling promises that she had made during the campaign, she worked hard to bring jobs and economic benefits to the upstate New York communities that had helped her win the election. She sponsored legislation to extend unemployment insurance to people who had lost their jobs; supported a farm bill that helped New York's $3.4 billion agriculture industry; and she hosted the first broadband conference in Canandaigua, New York, a small town in the Finger Lakes region. The conference helped bring better broadband Internet access to that part of the state.

"Senator Clinton is dedicated to bringing jobs to Upstate New York," wrote organizers of a software summit that Hillary attended. "Through tax credits for small businesses, investments in telecommunications infrastructure . . . and lowering airfares to increase regional accessibility, she proposes to make it possible for the economy in upstate and all regions of New York to flourish and to stem the outmigration of young New Yorkers and their families."[96]

Hillary also pursued legislation to champion the causes of children and education. She worked hard to reinstate a "Pediatric Rule" on medicines that had lapsed, which ensured that all medicines and vaccines were safe for children. She introduced legislation to rebuild schools, and she lobbied her fellow senators tirelessly to ensure new funding for teachers and underprivileged children. She was also able to secure legislation to provide $25 million for Internet Crimes Against Children task forces in every state.

In June 2001 Hillary's friend Jesse Jackson led a protest in Illinois against racial profiling, the practice of some police departments of singling out black and Hispanic people for questioning, ticketing, and criminal investigations. Shortly afterward Hillary cosponsored the End to Racial Profiling Act of 2001, which would ban the practice nationwide and punish police departments that engaged in the practice. As a *Newsweek* reporter noted about the freshman senator, "When she sees injustice, she fights it, which is what we should want in our leaders."[97]

RESPONDING TO THE SEPTEMBER 11 TERRORIST ATTACKS

On September 11, 2001, everything changed in American politics, and for Hillary in particular, when terrorists attacked the United

"We Will Not Be Caught Off Guard"

Pledging a new emphasis on homeland security in this 2003 speech that was posted on her official Senate website, http://clinton.senate.gov, Hillary called for Americans to be better prepared if future terrorist attacks occur:

"We want to show the terrorists that if they attack, we're prepared. We will not be caught off guard. We want to send a message that while they might break our hearts by taking away our loved ones, they will not break our spirit and take away the lives we lead as Americans. We can do this by filling some of the major gaps left by September 11th, like tracking the health of the first soldiers in this new war who lived and worked and volunteered at Ground Zero and coordinating our relief services."

States, killing thousands of people in New York City, Washington, D.C., and Pennsylvania and destroying New York's World Trade Center towers.

Hillary arrived from Washington at the scene of the wreckage in New York the day after the bombings. She called it "the most personally horrendous experience" of her life, adding, "This was beyond anything I've ever seen or imagined. I was totally unprepared for what I saw. The damage, the mountain of burning wreckage, the smell, just was overwhelming."[98]

Hillary helped comfort the families and victims of the tragedy, but she realized that the best thing she could do was to commit herself to gaining reparations in the Senate for the horrendous human and economic damage that had been done. She saw that responding to the emergency would dominate her agenda in the Senate for years to come, and she immediately got to work on the problem. "My job first and foremost has to be to try to make sure that all those people didn't die in vain and that whatever has to be done to protect us in the future and to rebuild New York . . . is all I'm doing and all I'm thinking about,"[99] she said.

To that end Hillary worked to secure $21.4 billion in funding for cleanup and recovery of the shattered World Trade Center area. She also moved quickly to provide health care tracking to the first people who responded to the attacks and to the volunteers who worked at Ground Zero directly after the attacks. She wanted to make sure that their health would be monitored long after the cleanup was completed. She saw that many small businesses in lower Manhattan were also devastated by the effects of the attacks, and she worked to provide funding for grants to keep them from going bankrupt.

When the 108th Congress began in 2003, Hillary's focus remained on homeland and national security. She was named to the Senate Committee on Armed Services and continued to serve on the two previous committees to which she had been initially named. On the Armed Services Committee, she concentrated on emergency preparedness and issues related to preparing for emerging threats. One of her first acts in the new Congress was to introduce the Homeland Security Block Grant Fund, which would provide direct funding for police officers, firefighters, emergency response personnel, and public health officials.

In just a few short years Hillary had gone from being a first lady in a White House that was tainted by scandal and suspicions to being a U.S. senator who was quickly becoming known as an effective legislator and powerful advocate for her constituency in New York. As Senator Barbara Mikulski of Maryland noted, Hillary "made it clear that she wanted to be a senator, not a celebrity."[100] Added husband Bill, "I'm so proud of her. I'm grateful that after all

Hillary Rodham Clinton visits the site of the 2001 World Trade Center attack. There, she spoke with rescue workers, comforted victims, and pledged to secure federal money for cleanup and recovery.

In this July 2003 photo, Senator Clinton autographs copies of her best-selling memoir Living History, in which she discusses her years as first lady.

the help she gave me for 27 years, I can now support her."[101]

ANOTHER FIRST FOR HILLARY

Of all of the firsts that Hillary, the former first lady, has accomplished, there is one first that is tantalizingly above all the rest. Friends and admirers have said for years that Hillary could run for president and that she possesses the unique skills and poise to become the first woman president in the country's history. She continues to be a leading presence in the Democratic Party, with a high approval rating among her constituents in New York. She has also proven to be a powerful fund-raiser, bringing in millions of dollars of donations to the Democratic

Party's coffers. "She's a star," said one political observer in Washingon. "She galvanizes democrats who saw her as a strong presence in the White House."[102]

Will she pursue the highest seat in the land? Hillary has ruled out running in the 2004 elections, citing her promise to serve out her entire six-year term in the Senate. But she has not ruled out entering the presidential campaign of 2008. When the question is raised as to whether she wants to run for the highest office in the land, Hillary has responded with a wink and a smile. "We'll talk later,"[103] she answers.

Notes

Introduction: A First Lady Like No Other

1. Quoted in Claire G. Osborne, ed., *The Unique Voice of Hillary Rodham Clinton.* New York: Avon Books, 1997.
2. Michael Tomasky, *Hillary's Turn: Inside Her Improbable, Victorious Senate Campaign.* New York: Free Press, 2001.

Chapter 1: A Daughter of High Expectations

3. Quoted in Osborne, *The Unique Voice of Hillary Rodham Clinton.*
4. Donnie Radcliffe, *Hillary Rodham Clinton: A First Lady for Our Time.* New York: Warner Books, 1993.
5. Quoted in Radcliffe, *Hillary Rodham Clinton.*
6. Gail Sheehy, *Hillary's Choice.* New York: Random House, 1999.
7. Quoted in Osborne, *The Unique Voice of Hillary Rodham Clinton.*
8. Quoted in Landon Y. Jones Jr. and Garry Clifford, "Bill Clinton & Hillary Rodham Clinton," *People Weekly,* December 28, 1992–January 4, 1993.
9. Quoted in Sheehy, *Hillary's Choice.*
10. Quoted in Sheehy, *Hillary's Choice.*
11. Quoted in Osborne, *The Unique Voice of Hillary Rodham Clinton.*
12. Joyce Milton, *The First Partner: Hillary Rodham Clinton.* New York: William Morrow, 1999.
13. Quoted in Radcliffe, *Hillary Rodham Clinton.*
14. Quoted in Sheehy, *Hillary's Choice.*
15. Quoted in Radcliffe, *Hillary Rodham Clinton.*
16. Quoted in Radcliffe, *Hillary Rodham Clinton.*

Chapter 2: The Making of an Activist

17. Quoted in Radcliffe, *Hillary Rodham Clinton.*
18. Sheehy, *Hillary's Choice.*
19. Quoted in Radcliffe, *Hillary Rodham Clinton.*
20. Sheehy, *Hillary's Choice.*
21. Quoted in Sheehy, *Hillary's Choice.*
22. Quoted in Osborne, *The Unique Voice of Hillary Rodham Clinton.*
23. Quoted in "Hillary Rodham Clinton," White House official website, www.whitehouse.gov.
24. Quoted in Radcliffe, *Hillary Rodham Clinton.*
25. Quoted in *Life,* "Protest Is an Attempt to Forge an Identity," June 20, 1969.
26. Quoted in Osborne, *The Unique Voice of Hillary Rodham Clinton.*
27. Radcliffe, *Hillary Rodham Clinton.*
28. Milton, *The First Partner.*
29. Quoted in Osborne, *The Unique Voice of Hillary Rodham Clinton.*
30. Quoted in Radcliffe, *Hillary Rodham Clinton.*
31. Quoted in Radcliffe, *Hillary Rodham Clinton.*
32. Quoted in Sheehy, *Hillary's Choice.*
33. Quoted in Radcliffe, *Hillary Rodham Clinton: A First Lady for Our Time.*

Chapter 3: Northern Style Meets Southern Politics

34. Radcliffe, *Hillary Rodham Clinton.*

35. Quoted in Osborne, *The Unique Voice of Hillary Rodham Clinton.*

36. Quoted in Osborne, *The Unique Voice of Hillary Rodham Clinton.*

37. Quoted in Radcliffe, *Hillary Rodham Clinton.*

38. Quoted in Milton, *The First Partner.*

39. Radcliffe, *Hillary Rodham Clinton.*

40. Quoted in Osborne, *The Unique Voice of Hillary Rodham Clinton.*

41. Quoted in Radcliffe, *Hillary Rodham Clinton.*

42. Sheehy, *Hillary's Choice.*

43. *Time*, "Southern Star Rising Again," September 20, 1982.

44. Quoted in Radcliffe, *Hillary Rodham Clinton.*

45. Quoted in Osborne, *The Unique Voice of Hillary Rodham Clinton.*

46. Quoted in *Time*, "Southern Star Rising Again."

47. Quoted in Osborne, *The Unique Voice of Hillary Rodham Clinton.*

48. Quoted in Radcliffe, *Hillary Rodham Clinton.*

49. Quoted in Sheehy, *Hillary's Choice.*

50. Quoted in Radcliffe, *Hillary Rodham Clinton.*

Chapter 4: The Two-for-One Presidency

51. Gail Sheehy, "What Hillary Wants," *Vanity Fair*, May 1991.

52. Quoted in Sheehy, "What Hillary Wants."

53. Margaret Carlson, "A Different Kind of First Lady," *Time*, November 16, 1992.

54. Sheehy, *Hillary's Choice.*

55. Quoted in Donnie Radcliffe, *Hillary Rodham Clinton.*

56. Quoted in "Hillary Rodham Clinton."

57. Quoted in Margaret Carlson, "All Eyes on Hillary," *Time*, September 14, 1992.

58. Quoted in Carlson, "A Different Kind of First Lady."

59. Quoted in Sheehy, "What Hillary Wants."

60. Margaret Carlson, "A Hundred Days of Hillary," *Vanity Fair*, June 1993.

61. Carlson, "A Hundred Days of Hillary."

62. James Fallows, "A Triumph of Misinformation," *Atlantic Monthly*, January 1995.

63. Quoted in "Biography of Senator Hillary Rodham Clinton," New York Software Industry Association, www.nysia.org.

64. Milton, *The First Partner.*

65. Hillary Rodham Clinton, *It Takes a Village: And Other Lessons Children Teach Us.* New York: Simon & Schuster, 1996.

66. Quoted in Jones and Clifford, "Bill Clinton & Hillary Rodham Clinton."

67. Clinton, *It Takes a Village.*

68. Hillary Rodham Clinton, *An Invitation to the White House: At Home with History.* New York: Simon & Schuster, 2000.

69. Quoted in Sheehy, *Hillary's Choice.*

Chapter 5: Scandal and Denial

70. Quoted in Radcliffe, *Hillary Rodham Clinton.*

71. Quoted in Osborne, *The Unique Voice of Hillary Rodham Clinton.*

72. Quoted in Osborne, *The Unique Voice of Hillary Rodham Clinton.*

73. *Newsweek*, "Hillary's Trouble," March 14, 1994

74. Leslie Bennetts, "Pinning Down Hillary," *Vanity Fair*, June 1994.

75. Quoted in Bennetts, "Pinning Down Hillary."

76. *Newsweek*, "Hillary's Trouble."

77. Quoted in Osborne, *The Unique Voice of Hillary Rodham Clinton.*

78. Quoted in Michael Duffy, "Open and

Unflappable," *Time*, May 2, 1994.

79. Quoted in Eleanor Clift, "Hillary: 'I Made Mistakes,'" *Newsweek*, March 21, 1994.
80. Quoted in Clift, "Hillary: 'I Made Mistakes.'"
81. Quoted in Sheehy, *Hillary's Choice.*
82. Quoted in Milton, *The First Partner.*
83. Quoted in Associated Press, "In Book Hillary Clinton Details Pain from Affair," June 4, 2003.
84. Quoted in Associated Press, "In Book Hillary Clinton Details Pain from Affair."
85. Sheehy, *Hillary's Choice.*

Chapter 6: Senator Clinton

86. Quoted in Milton, *The First Partner.*
87. Tomasky, *Hillary's Turn.*
88. Quoted in Tomasky, *Hillary's Turn.*
89. Quoted in Adam Nagourney, "Hillary Clinton Begins Pre-Campaign in a New Role for Her," *New York Times*, July 8, 1999.
90. Elizabeth Kolbert, "Running on Empathy," *New Yorker*, February 7, 2000.
91. Quoted in Kolbert, "Running on Empathy."
92. Tomasky, *Hillary's Turn.*
93. Quoted in Kolbert, "Running on Empathy."
94. Tomasky, *Hillary's Turn.*
95. Quoted in "Newsmakers: Hillary Rodham Clinton," ABC News, www.abc-news. go.com.
96. Quoted in "Biography of Senator Hillary Rodham Clinton."
97. Jonathan Alter, "Hillary Raises Her Profile," *Newsweek*, June 25, 2001.
98. Quoted in *Washington Post*, "Clinton: Damage 'Incalculable,'" October 11, 2001.
99. Quoted in *Washington Post*, "Clinton: Damage 'Incalculable.'"
100. Quoted in *People Weekly*, "Hillary, Act II," July 1, 2002.
101. Quoted in *People Weekly*, "Hillary, Act II."
102. *People Weekly*, "Hillary, Act II."
103. Quoted in Sheehy, *Hillary's Choice.*

For Further Reading

Books

JoAnn Bren Guernsey, *Hillary Rodham Clinton: A New Kind of First Lady.* Minneapolis: Lerner, 1993. Guernsey paints a sympathetic portrait of Hillary as a strong woman who was frequently vilified by the public in this biography aimed at younger readers.

Patrick S. Halley, *On the Road with Hillary.* New York: Viking Penguin, 2002. A key member of Hillary's advance team (which coordinated all of her appearances around the country and the world), author Halley tells engaging stories about the behind-the-scenes workings of Hillary's public appearances from the presidential campaign of 1992 to her election to the U.S. Senate.

Richard Kozar, *Hillary Rodham Clinton.* Philadelphia: Chelsea House, 1998. In this book aimed at young-adult readers, Kozar portrays Hillary's life in the context of the times in which she grew up and alongside the lives and careers of other high-achieving women throughout history.

Jerry Oppenheimer, *State of a Union.* New York: HarperCollins, 2000. Investigative biographer Oppenheimer dug deep through interviews with friends and associates of the Clintons to forge this revealing, intimate, and sometimes bawdy portrait of their complex marriage. The book gives details about the collegiate Bill and Hillary (such as his passion for eating and her compassion for young men in the armed forces draft).

Websites

Whilte House Website (www.whitehouse. gov). The White House's official website has biographical information on all of the presidents and first ladies, including Hillary.

Hillary Rodham Clinton Senate Website (http://clinton.senate.gov). Senator Hillary Rodham Clinton's official website has extensive biographical information about Hillary's life, as well as up-to-date reports of her speeches and the issues that she is addressing. Links provide access to her legislative record.

Works Consulted

Books

Hillary Rodham Clinton, *An Invitation to the White House: At Home with History*. New York: Simon & Schuster, 2000. Hillary wrote this oversized book as a tribute to the White House itself. It contains many photographs of the White House's public rooms and offers inside looks at the inner workings of the famous mansion.

Hillary Rodham Clinton, *It Takes a Village: And Other Lessons Children Teach Us*. New York: Simon & Schuster, 1996. Hillary's first book as first lady called upon the community of parents, neighbors, and professional caregivers to provide a peaceful, safe, and nurturing environment for all children.

Joyce Milton, *The First Partner: Hillary Rodham Clinton*. New York: William Morrow, 1999. An unflinching and sometimes critical biography of Hillary, with in-depth research of the Whitewater and Travelgate scandals.

Claire G. Osborne, ed. *The Unique Voice of Hillary Rodham Clinton*. New York: Avon Books, 1997. This collection of quotes by Hillary was compiled from dozens of interviews that she gave, and provides concise information of Hillary's views on topics ranging from her childhood days in Illinois to the role of women in societies around the world.

Donnie Radcliffe, *Hillary Rodham Clinton: A First Lady for Our Time*. New York: Warner Books, 1993. A sympathetic and well-written biography of Hillary written during her first year as first lady, with an interesting interview at the end of the book that the author held with Hillary during a flight on *Air Force One*.

Gail Sheehy, *Hillary's Choice*. New York: Random House, 1999. The noted author and journalist gathered information from several of her *Vanity Fair* magazine profiles of Hillary and interviewed dozens of people from Hillary's past to compile this authoritative biography of the first lady, which was published at the height of the Monica Lewinsky scandal.

Michael Tomasky, *Hillary's Turn: Inside Her Improbable, Victorious Senate Campaign*. New York: Free Press, 2001. The author, a political reporter for *New York* magazine, followed Hillary's campaign for U.S. Senator in this engaging and fast-moving account, which is loaded with information on the inner workings of New York State politics.

Periodicals

Jonathan Alter, "Hillary Raises Her Profile," *Newsweek*, June 25, 2001.

Associated Press, "In Book, Hillary Clinton Details Pain From Affair," June 4, 2003.

Leslie Bennetts, "Pinning Down Hillary," *Vanity Fair,* June 1994.

Margaret Carlson, "A Different Kind of First Lady," *Time*, November 16, 1992.

Margaret Carlson, "A Hundred Days of Hillary," *Vanity Fair*, June 1993.

Margaret Carlson, "All Eyes on Hillary," *Time*, September 14, 1992.

Eleanor Clift, "Hillary: 'I Made Mistakes,'" *Newsweek*, March 21, 1994.

Michael Duffy, "Open and Unflappable," *Time*, May 2, 1994.

James Fallows, "A Triumph of Misinformation," *Atlantic Monthly*, January 1995.

Landon Y. Jones Jr. and Garry Clifford, "Bill Clinton & Hillary Rodham Clinton," *People Weekly*, December 28, 1992–January 4, 1993.

Elizabeth Kolbert, "Running on Empathy," *New Yorker*, February 7, 2000.

Life, "Protest Is an Attempt to Forge an Identity," June 20, 1969.

Adam Nagourney, "Hillary Clinton Begins Pre-Campaign in a New Role for Her," *New York Times*, July 8, 1999.

Newsweek, "Hillary's Trouble," March 14, 1994.

People Weekly, "Hillary, Act II," July 1, 2002.

Gail Sheehy, "What Hillary Wants," *Vanity Fair*, May 1991.

Time, "Southern Star Rising Again," September 20, 1982.

Washington Post, "Clinton: Damage 'Incalculable,'" October 11, 2001.

Internet Sources

"Biography of Senator Hillary Rodham Clinton." New York Software Industry Association, www.nysia.org. This biographical sketch of Hillary, written for a software summit in upstate New York that Hillary attended in 2002, summarizes her early work as a U.S. Senator.

"Hillary Rodham Clinton." White House official website, www.whitehouse.gov. The White House website contains biographical information on all past presidents and first ladies, including this warm summary of Hillary's stint in the White House.

"Newsmakers: Hillary Rodham Clinton." ABC News, www.abcnews.go.com. A summary of Hillary's life and accomplishments up to her victory in the U.S. Senate campaign of 1999 on this portion of the *ABC News* website that is devoted to biographical sketches of important people.

Index

Picture Credits

Cover photo: © Lorenzo Ciniglio/CORBIS SYGMA

AP/Wide World Photos, 24, 47, 52, 55, 67, 70, 77, 87, 89, 93

Courtesy Arkansas History Commission, 50

Burton Berinsky/Landov, 44

© Bettmann/CORBIS, 30, 33

© CORBIS SYGMA, 37

Getty Images, 46, 61, 79

Gary Hershorn/Reuters/Landov, 12

© Brooks Kraft/CORBIS SYGMA, 26, 42

Library of Congress, 58

© Wally McNamee/CORBIS, 36

© Wally McNamee/CORBIS SYGMA, 73

Win McNamee/Reuters/Landov, 65

Reuters/Landov, 70

Reuters NewMedia Inc./CORBIS, 92

Mike Segar/Reuters/Landov, 85, 88

© Jerry Staley/CORBIS SYGMA, 15

© Mike Stewart/CORBIS SYGMA, 40

Ray Stubblebine/Reuters/Landov, 83

UPI/Landov, 21

Bruce Young/Reuters/Landov, 63

Steve Zmina, 18

About the Author

Author Jim Gullo grew up in the Finger Lakes region of New York State and lived in New York City for several years after graduating from the University of Arizona with a degree in journalism. He is the co-author, with Charlie Sifford, of *Just Let Me Play: The Story of Charlie Sifford,* an autobiography of African American golf pioneer Sifford, and the guidebook *Seattle & Portland for Dummies.* He now lives in Seattle with his wife, Kris, and two sons, Michael and Joe.